A Word About Recipe Donors

In this age of 17,000-mile-an-hour satellites, many wonderful people in the California wine industry still take time to put together taste treats that would have brought ecstasy to Epicurus himself—the founder of the Epicurean movement.

To bring you recipes that would qualify as Epicurean, we appealed to the winemakers of California, their wives and those associated with them in wine production, promotion, sales and research.

We asked them to send in those recipes for wine cookery that they, their families and friends found so delightful as to be worthy of preparation over and over again.

The experience and discriminating taste of flavor-conscious cooks will be detected in both the simple and complicated recipes that make up this unusual Epicurean collection to which they contributed.

They also shared with us one or more specific choices of wines to accompany each main dish as a table beverage. Following their selections will prove what every vintner knows—that wine-cooked foods accompanied by compatible and complementary vinous beverages can change an ordinary dinner into a banquet and an ordinary banquet into a feast.

We know from our previous books, *Favorite Recipes of California Winemakers* and *Adventures in Wine Cookery by California Winemakers* that our contributors receive many complimentary letters from those who read and use their recipes.

To the warm, friendly appreciation that most likely will be forthcoming from readers, let us add our sincere thanks to California winemakers, their friends and associates for sending us the recipes that made this book possible.

D. C. Turrentine, Manager
WINE ADVISORY BOARD
717 Market Street
San Francisco, Calif. 94103

Epicurean Recipes
of California Winemakers

by Wine Advisory Board

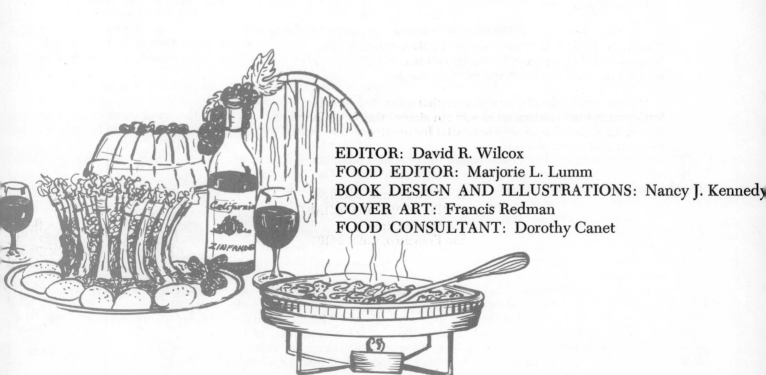

EDITOR: David R. Wilcox
FOOD EDITOR: Marjorie L. Lumm
BOOK DESIGN AND ILLUSTRATIONS: Nancy J. Kennedy
COVER ART: Francis Redman
FOOD CONSULTANT: Dorothy Canet

Wine and Food for Epicures
...a matter of taste

by Marjorie L. Lumm

There are a number of definitions of "Epicurean." We like the one which says ". . . suited to an Epicure," along with the definition of an Epicure as ". . . one with discriminating tastes in food and wine." This is the sense in which Epicurean is used in this book.

The word Epicurean came from Epicurus, a Greek philosopher who lived and taught in the vicinity of Athens in the third century, B.C. The school he established was set in a garden. There he lived with his pupils. The society which he gathered around him included women as well as men, a circumstance which occasioned some scandalous legends.

History records his unsurpassed kindness to all, and the simplicity which characterized the regimen of his school.

The philosophic outlook of Epicurus was fundamentally ethical. Even his interest in physics was to obtain a theory of life which "shall insure quietude of mind and a steadfast faith." He taught that a right conception of pleasure itself induces to right living, because it is not possible to live pleasantly without living wisely and well and righteously.

Thus the appreciation of foods and wines which we term "Epicurean" and regard as very much a part of today's scene, is actually as old as written history. Since the days of Epicurus, Epicurean wining and dining has fallen and risen often through many cultural changes—climbing when times were good, when man had leisure and means, and falling when there were wars or hardships. In the past this art has oftentimes been limited to the few who had the means and the time to devote to it.

Now our affluent society is fostering a more extensive interest in foods and wine than at any other period of history. A much larger segment of the population of America now has the interest and the time to practice the art of good living. The enjoyment of food and wine need be limited only by our knowledge and our taste.

"Epicurean" connotes validity—the honest use of honest products, and a feeling for the harmony of wines and foods. These are cultivated tastes. This is knowledge pleasantly come by through experience. The recipes in this book and the suggestions for matching them with wines are guides to enjoyment and the good life.

Modern agriculture and our fast distribution systems make the finest products of the world easily available to us in one convenient form or another. It takes the discernment of an Epicure more than a generous purse to choose the freshest vegetables, the quality and cut of meat best suited to the occasion, and the wines to complement them.

The practice of the art of good living means giving the same attention to our daily food and drink that we would give to a company meal. Selecting the foods and wines is the first step. Preparing them for the table is the next. Both are equally important. Both benefit from experience. Sometimes the best combination of ingredients, the most skillful method of putting them together, the most suitable equipment and cooking methods come after doing a recipe several times. And once the food is perfect, there is the art of presenting it most attractively.

From start to finish, it's a fascinating process, with continuing opportunities for change and improvement.

Table of Contents

Recipes

The ABC's of VINTAGE YEARS

The question comes up now and then: Does California have vintage years, or doesn't it? The answer, as all good answers must be, is yes and no.

A grapevine is a fussy plant. It reacts to minor changes in its environment. Each new season, in California or anywhere else, each vine produces a different grape than it did the year before. And, since a wine depends in large part on the grapes that go into it, there are inevitable differences in the wines from each year to the next.

The thing about California is that its winemakers expect a vintage every year—year in and year out. They differ from their European counterparts in this. Some years (1968, for one) European vintners endure vintages they would just as soon forget. It is this which has aroused the mystique of the vintage.

In its broadest definition, a vintage year is one which produces ripe grapes. There is an absolute relationship between the amount of natural sugar in the grape and the level of alcohol that fermentation will produce from it. A wine too low in alcohol, from a "poor" vintage, will not amount to much. This calamity does not befall California's vintners. When it happens to other vintners, they are apt to add non-grape sugar during fermentation to increase the alcohol to a normal level.

In narrow definitions, vintage years depend on more subtle details in the grape's development—color intensity, sugar-acid ratios, and other technical considerations. These minor variations produce varying characteristics. The Cabernet Sauvignon from a cool year, say, is likely to produce a powerful, long-lived wine that takes some time to reach its best. The same grape in a warmer year will yield a wine that will be soft and agreeable much sooner after the harvest.

The winemaker can choose between two basic alternatives in these aspects of a vintage year. He can elect to make a "vintage" wine—which in California means it is made entirely from the grapes of a single harvest and labelled as being of that year. Or he can blend in some wines of two or three years earlier to smooth out differences and so offer wine that is much the same year after year, no matter how capricious the summer sun. Happily, there are different winemakers who choose to do each (and sometimes both). This offers the Epicure a greater range of wines to choose among, and assures him of wines ready for drinking now, and after five or more years of patient waiting.

Vintages apply almost exclusively to table wines. Dessert wines—with the rare exception of some Ports and sparkling wines—usually are blended from several different vintages in order to have both new and aged flavors contribute to the character of these elixirs.

How to Read a Wine Label

A WHITE DINNER WIN
Pinot Blanc
ALCOHOL 12½% BY VOLUME
PRODUCED AND BOTTLED IN
California
WINELAND OF AMER

One of the joys in creating an Epicurean meal is selecting the wines. This takes some time and thought, just as menu-planning does. But perfect pairings of wines and foods are basic to truly memorable meals.

Wine selection is easier when the art of label-reading is well in hand. This is uncomplicated business in the case of California wines.

All California wine labels state the origin of the bottle contents prominently. The word "California" itself tells a lot about the wine. It automatically guarantees that every drop in the bottle was made from the juice of pure, fresh grapes grown and fermented in California. No water added. No sugar. No other non-grape substance of any kind.

The only exceptions are sparkling and special natural flavored wines, including Vermouth. A bit of sugar or sugar-syrup may be added to promote second fermentation (the one which puts the bubbles in sparkling wines) and to control the sweetness. With flavored wines, sugar may be added, as well as citrus, coffee, or other special natural essences that give the wine its particular character. Otherwise, only the grapes themselves provide the sweetness and alcohol present in California wines.

As for more definitive vineyard locations, a California bottle naming "Fair Valley" on the label must contain at least 75% of wine grown in that valley. In the same way, at least 75% of a wine labeled "Mountain" red or white must come from grapes grown in mountainous regions or on hillsides.

The winery name on a California label may be preceded by the words "Produced and Bottled By" or "Made and Bottled By." "Produced" means that at least 75% of the wine was crushed, fermented, and finished by the bottler. "Made" means that generally 10% of the wine was made by the bottler. In either case, the vintner considered the wine worthy of his name and representative of his skill.

If a California wine has a varietal name—Cabernet Sauvignon, Pinot Blanc, etc.—at least 51% of the wine must be made from the grape variety named on the label. (The figure is usually much higher, frequently 100% of the variety.) The wine must also display the predominant taste, aroma, and characteristics of that grape variety.

A generic designation like Claret, Burgundy, Sherry, Rhine wine, Chablis, Sauterne, Chianti, or Rosé is more general. This kind of labeling describes a California wine type in broad terms varying from vintner to vintner.

Some California labels show vintage dates. When this happens, all of the grapes used in the wine were harvested and crushed during the year named.

Alcoholic content is also shown on California wine labels in percentage by volume. In appetizer and dessert wines, the alcoholic content ranges from 19.5 to 21 percent; except Vermouths and special natural wines may be lower. Table wines contain an alcoholic content varying from 10% to 14% by volume—the percentage is always shown on the label.

GENERICS

Generics are named for districts which originally produced wines with similar characteristics.

WHITE WINES

Most preferred chilled with fish, shellfish, poultry. Usual serving—4 ounces.
Light, medium dry white wines, ranging in color from pale golden to slightly green-gold.

Rhine Wine   **White Chianti**

Rich, distinctive whites with full flavor and a pale or light gold color. These wines are dry, often fruity.

Chablis   Dry Sauterne   Mountain White

Medium sweet to quite sweet wines. Especially good with desserts, fruits, fruit salad, and other sweet foods.

Haut Sauterne   Sweet Sauterne
Light Muscat   "Chateau" White Wines

ROSÉ WINES

Most preferred chilled with ham, pork, veal, lamb, poultry. Usual serving—4 ounces.
These wines are light and fruity, usually medium-dry. They're ideal picnic and luncheon wines.

Vin Rosé   **Rosé**

STORING WINE. Air and light are wine's enemies. Good home storage conditions for wine are found in closets, drawers, cupboards, and cellars where it is cool and dark. Lay corked bottles on their sides to keep the corks moist and tight. Screw cap bottles can be safely stored upright.

RED WINES

Most preferred at cool room temperature with steaks, roasts, game, spaghetti, cheeses, stews, casseroles. Usual serving—4 ounces.
Dry wines, from light red to deep ruby in color, often pleasantly tart, with medium to full body.

Burgundy   **Claret**
Chianti   **Mountain Red**

Mellow reds, of medium body with just a touch of sweetness and a pleasing, hearty flavor.

Barberone   **Vino-Rosso**

PROPRIETARIES: Other red, white, and rosé dinner wines are labeled with special names selected by the winemaker. These proprietary names may be coined or descriptive words, sometimes indicating the region in which the wine was produced. Proprietary wines parallel Generics in range and use.

APPETIZER WINES

Aperitif or appetizer wines are usually dry and are drunk before meals or with the soup course. Chill them, or serve at room temperature, or pour over ice. Usual serving—3 ounces.

Sherry   **Vermouth**
  Cocktail   Dry
  Dry   Sweet
  Medium Dry

DESSERT WINES

Pour dessert wines after dinner, either with dessert or later. They are all sweet, rich wines that are particularly good with fruit, nuts, cheese, plain cake, cookies. Dessert wines are usually served at room temperature. Usual serving—3 ounces.

Port   **Angelica**
  Ruby   **Cream Sherry**
  Tawny   **Madeira**
  Tinta   **Marsala**
  White   **Tokay**

Muscatel
  Black Muscat
  Muscat Frontignan
  Muscatel (gold or red)

Sweet Sauterne and Sweet Semillon are also often served as dessert wines.

WINES

WINES

(Dinner wines.)

VARIETALS

Varietals are named for the grapes from which they are made.

WHITE WINES

Most preferred chilled with fish, shellfish, poultry. Usual serving—4 ounces.
Light crisp white wines, pale golden or slightly green-gold in color. Most are pleasantly dry. Some may have a hint of sweetness.*

* *Emerald Riesling   Johannisberg Riesling
* *Gewurztraminer   (White Riesling)
* *Green Hungarian   Sylvaner
* Grey Riesling   Traminer

Rich, fuller-flavored wines. These are usually dry wines, pale to light golden in color. Some may have a hint of sweetness.*

* Chardonnay   *Chenin Blanc
* (Pinot Chardonnay)   (White Pinot)
* Pinot Blanc   Sauvignon Blanc
*   Dry Semillon

Medium to pronounced sweetness in these wines. They may be enjoyed most with dessert, fruit, fruit salad, and other sweet foods.

* Malvasia Bianca   Muscat Canelli
* Muscat Bordelaise   Sweet Semillon

ROSÉ WINES

Most preferred chilled with ham, pork, veal, lamb, poultry. Usual serving—4 ounces.
These are light, fruity wines, sometimes dry, sometimes slightly sweet,* with a cheerful pink color, ranging in tone from deep rose to a pale, orange-tinged hue.

* Cabernet Rosé   Gamay Rosé
* Grignolino Rosé   Zinfandel Rosé
*   *Grenache Rosé

SERVING WINE. Most people enjoy white and rosé wines chilled to about 45-55 degrees. An hour in the refrigerator will do it handily.

RED WINES

Most preferred at cool room temperature with steaks, roasts, game, spaghetti, cheeses, stews, casseroles. Usual serving—4 ounces.
Fresh, fruity red wines, dry and aromatic, light to medium in body.

* Cabernet   Gamay
* Grignolino   Gamay Beaujolais
* Pinot St. George   Ruby Cabernet
* (Red Pinot)   Zinfandel

Rich, red wines with distinctive flavor and appealing ruby color, medium to full in body.

* Barbara   Cabernet Sauvignon
* Charbono   Pinot Noir
*   Petite Sirah

SERVING WINE. Many wine drinkers agree that red wines benefit from a little "breathing time," and open them about an hour before dinner and leave the closure off. You may be pleased by the changes in aroma and flavor this short exposure gives the wine.

SPARKLING WINES

These festive wines are appropriate anytime, along with food or by themselves. They range from extremely dry to quite sweet, from pale gold to deep red. Sparkling wines are best when thoroughly chilled. Usual serving—3-4 ounces.

Champagne
   Natural—very dry
   Brut—dry
   Extra Dry — with just a hint of sweetness
   Dry — medium sweet
   Sec — noticeably sweet
   Demi-Sec — very sweet

Rosé
   Pink Champagne
   Crackling Rosé
Red
   Sparkling Burgundy
Muscat
   Sparkling Muscat

SERVING WINE. Traditionally, wine is served in clear, stemmed glasses, filled about half way. This leaves room for the aroma to gather above the wine. Winemakers recommend a tulip-shaped glass with an 8-9 ounce capacity as being suitable for any wine.

SPECIAL NATURAL WINES

These wines are pure, grape wines flavored with fruit juices or essences. Citrus flavors are especially popular, also mint, coffee, chocolate, and herbs. The wines are given descriptive or colorful names by the winemaker. They may be enjoyed before meals, with dessert, after dinner, or as between meal refreshments. Usual serving—3 ounces.

WINE ACCESSORIES

Many people who enjoy wine like to collect a selection of serving accouterments. Quite an array of glassware, coasters, corkscrews, and other equipment is available at a wide range of prices, making it possible for anyone interested to expand the household supply of wine gear.

Glasses are probably the most important wine items—aside from the bottles themselves. A clear, thin glass, designed especially to present wine attractively, compounds the pleasures of the beverage. Although wine cheers a table even when served in jelly glasses.

The wine growers of California agree that wine glasses should be plain and clear—the better to see the color of the wine. They should also be roomy, to allow for generous servings of wine, and tulip shaped, so the good wine aroma is captured in the glass above the wine. Wine growers also recommend glasses with stems. A stem acts as a sort of handle, keeping warm fingers away from chilled wine.

A single style glass will work well for all wines, if it is the 8–9 ounce, tulip-shaped, all-purpose wineglass recommended by both wine growers and connoisseurs. Or, a whole range of special glasses, a different one for each type of wine, may be collected. Hostesses who prefer the array may set the table with conical or elongated-tulip Sherry glasses, round-bowled hock glasses, classic red and white Burgundy glasses, Claret glasses, saucer-shaped or tulip Champagne glasses, in any combination that fits the meal and wine list. There is no question about the aura of elegance surrounding a table laden with shining crystal wine-glasses, each place set with a separate glowing vessel for every wine presented during the meal. But the simpler solution of a single all-purpose glass is perfectly proper and commands less table space.

Outsized glasses are the special pleasure of wine lovers. These Burgundy balloons or enormous Bordeaux glasses allow the connoisseur to swirl his wine enthusiastically without spilling a drop. Capacity is two or three times the usual 8–9 ounce all-purpose wine glass. These glasses seem to emphasize the presence of wine and dramatize a table setting.

Dinner tables are also enhanced by wine coasters. Many are made of silver or are silver-plated. Others are crockery, wood, pewter, straw, or what-have-you. They come in sizes just right for ordinary 4/5 quart bottles, or larger to accommodate magnum or Champagne bottles. These devices serve a practical purpose, as well as a decorative one. They protect the table linen.

Another item which serves this same end is the drip-stopper. It's usually made of silver and fits snugly in the top of the wine bottle. The drip-stopper assures neat pouring, even by novices.

Wine coolers may add to the enjoyment of chilled wines. A silver bucket, beaded with moisture and exhibiting a chilled bottle, lends a special authority to the wine and a festive note to the table. Practically speaking, a cooler assures a host of pouring white or sparkling wines at a desirable serving temperature throughout the whole meal.

An effective, easy-to-use corkscrew is one of the most important pieces of equipment a wine lover can own. Although many wines come in screwcap bottles, eliminating the need for corkscrews entirely, a corkscrew is still a necessary tool for removing the barrier between many wines and the people who want to drink them. There are almost limitless shapes and sizes of corkscrews. But the thing to pay attention to when selecting one is the length and turn of the screw. The helix (screw portion) should be long enough to penetrate all the way through any cork likely to be used in a wine bottle. 2¼ inches should do it. And the coil should follow the path set by the point exactly. A leverage device of some kind is a great advantage on a corkscrew.

An alternative to the classic corkscrew is a hand-pump cork remover. This little instrument features a needle attached to a plunger-type pump. It's easy to use. Just insert the needle in the cork, pump the plunger two or three times, and out pops the cork. A similar cork remover using Freon gas with a very slight touch does the same job with less effort. But careful! A heavy touch can cause trouble.

Carafes and decanters are other wine items which bring pleasure to the table. These containers are generally graceful in shape, attractive in design. They may be simple or elaborate. Carafes come without lids and are useful for holding meal-size quantities of wine poured from gallon or half gallon jugs. Most decanters have stoppers and are the traditional sideboard containers for displaying the family Port or Sherry. They are also meant to hold old, sediment-filled wine which must be decanted, or poured from the original bottle into another clean receptacle, leaving the sediment behind. When this purpose is to be served, a decanter with a wide mouth eases the delicate job of pouring without disturbing sediment.

Some special wine equipment is meant for outdoor use. The bota is one such item. It is a hide bag, Spanish in origin. The bota is the skier's and hiker's friend. It is lightweight and unbreakable, ideal for carrying wine along on outdoor sojourns.

Another outdoor item is the plastic wine glass. Because it doesn't shatter, this kind of glass is perfect for poolside use. It is also inexpensive. Large parties indoors or out may be more pleasant for the hostess who uses these throw-away plastic glasses instead of regular wine glasses.

Most of these accompaniments to wine drinking can be found easily in gift or department stores. If a desirable item is not available in your area, write to Wine Advisory Board, 717 Market Street, San Francisco 94103, for help in locating it.

Wine As a Food

By Salvatore P. Lucia, M.D.

Professor Emeritus of Medicine, University of California School of Medicine

Wine was a safe and healthful beverage from the very beginning of early civilizations. It provided calories and vitamins before the science of nutrition was established, and at a time when food was neither plentiful nor always of good quality. During those times when life was physically strenuous, wine offered the tranquility and relaxation necessary to bind societies of men together, as well as to lessen tensions and relieve pain.

Health Laden Elixir

In time, the dietary alcoholic beverage, wine, came to be esteemed in its own right as a health-laden elixir, bringing to man bounties which only now are being specifically identified and given a scientific verification. As a food, wine plays, in addition, an important role in present day nutrition. Wine contains many of the elements essential for quick energy and body maintenance, support, and repair. The energy element is derived largely from alcohol, a simple carbohydrate—the necessary substratum without which, wine would not be wine. This is balanced by organic and inorganic acids, other carbohydrates, vitamins, and a myriad of diverse congeners present in wine in varying proportion, depending upon the climate and soil of the vineyards, the variety of grapes, the degree of maturity of the grapes at harvest, the processes used in fermentation, aging and all the other operations well known to the maker of wine.

In addition to the alcohol, other sources of calories in wine are the simple sugars, principally levulose and dextrose, which occur in amounts of 0.25% to 10%, depending upon the type of wine. It has been shown that levulose acts in the maintenance and repair of the liver and as an intermediary substance in metabolism. Dextrose is considered the most important single factor in the prevention of fatty infiltration of the liver, a condition which predisposes this organ to cirrhosis.

B Vitamins

The vitamins in grapes are used primarily as accessory growth factors for micro-organisms although some of them are present in sufficient amount to be of importance in human nutrition. The B vitamins are represented fairly well in the grape, its musts and wines. In wines that were tested for B vitamins, Agnes Fay Morgan demonstrated that while low in thiamine content they provided 13 to 18% of the daily minimum requirement of riboflavin, 52 to 94% of pyridoxine, 5 to 14% of niacin, and 2 to 5% of pantothenic acid. Sweet red wines shelter much more of the thiamine, all of the riboflavin and niacin, 3/4 of the vitamin B_6 and 1/3 of the pantothenic acid present in the natural grape. The reasons for this better showing by sweet red wines may be due to the inclusion of the skins and seeds of the grapes during fermentation; the shorter fermentation period, as attested by the high sugar content of the wine; and to the shielding of the riboflavin from the destructive action of light by the heavy pigments in the wine. The presence of B vitamins in wine significantly distinguishes it from distilled liquors and even from beer. Not only original endowment of the grape, but the additions and subtractions produced in the fermented juice by the yeasts, must be taken into account in assessing the quality content of B vitamins in wines.

Tonic Action

Experiments have also revealed that wine has a remarkable vitamin P potency, a factor which may strengthen capillary resistance. Owing to the importance of the capillaries in the nutrition of tissues, the "tonic" action of wines can and should be attributed in considerable measure to their content of vitamin P.

As for minerals, wines contain in some degree all thirteen of the major mineral elements considered necessary for the maintenance of human life, i.e., calcium, phosphorous, magnesium, sodium, potassium, chlorine, sulphur, iron, copper, manganese, zinc, iodine, and cobalt.

Port wine has long been recommended in the treatment of iron-deficiency anemia, and for good reason, for it contains an average of 3.5 mg. of iron per liter—the daily requirement of elemental iron being 5.5 mg., according to the latest scientific findings. Other wines are richer still in iron, with an average of 4.7 mg. per liter for the dry white table wines and 6.0 mg. for the dry red table wines.

Wine in Cooking

Wine is a most versatile flavoring agent and adds "a gourmet touch" to any dish from appetizer to dessert. Wines packaged in gallon and half-gallon jugs are quite satisfactory for cooking as well as those in fifths and other bottle sizes.

Foods cooked with wine have the flavor of the wine without any residue of alcohol, because alcohol evaportes long before the cooking temperature of food is reached.

The plans for most Epicurean meals start with the main dish. So here, grouped for easy perusal, are recipes for wine-flavored meats, poultry and fish — any one of which may be the center of interest in an outstanding menu. The contributors of many of these recipes have listed the accompaniments they've found most compatible. A further menu planning aid is the suggestion of a California wine that complements each main dish.

Among the fish recipes are several that may serve as a separate fish course to precede the main course. When a multi-course menu will include two or more wines, tradition suggests that the wines for the first courses will be lighter in color, body and flavor than those that follow. The most robust wine of the meal — whether it be red or white — accompanies the main course.

MAIN DISHES

Beef Ragout

(6 TO 8 SERVINGS)

Mrs. Edmund Accomazzo, Cucamonga Winery, Cucamonga
Editor's note: This stew is excellently seasoned. Though the meat is not browned in advance, the long cooking gives it good color and flavor.

3 pounds boneless beef chuck, cut into 1-inch cubes
  Flour
1 (10½-oz.) can condensed consomme
½ cup California Dry Sherry
2 small onions, thinly sliced
½ teaspoon curry powder
¼ teaspoon dried basil leaves
1 whole clove
1 bay leaf
  Dash of garlic salt
  Dash freshly ground black pepper
½ strip bacon
1 coarse stalk celery
12 to 15 whole baby carrots, scraped and sliced
1 mint leaf or pinch of dried mint
4 small tomatoes, peeled and cubed
½ pound sliced fresh mushrooms or
1 (6-oz.) can slice mushrooms, drained
2 tablespoons flour
1 (8 oz.) can tomato puree
½ cup finely chopped celery
½ cup finely chopped parsley

Roll beef pieces in flour to coat evenly. Place meat, consomme, Sherry onions, curry powder, basil leaves, clove, bay leaf, garlic salt and pepper in an ovenproof Dutch oven. Place over moderate heat (about 250°) and heat until mixture begins to boil. Add the bacon and celery stalk. Cover Dutch oven and place in a preheated 350° oven. Bake about 2 hours, or until meat is fork-tender. While meat is cooking, place carrots and mint leaf in a saucepan. Add about 1 cup water. Place over moderately low heat and cook 10 to 15 minutes or until tender. Drain. When meat is fork-tender, take Dutch oven out of oven and remove bacon and celery stalk Place oven over moderate heat. Add tomatoes and mushrooms; sprinkle the 2 tablespoons flour over mixture and stir to blend. Simmer, covered, 10 to 15 minutes. Add cooked carrots, tomato puree, the chopped celery and parsley and stir to blend. Season to taste with salt and pepper.

*Editor's Note: Any **CALIFORNIA RED TABLE WINE** would go well with this dish.*

15

Braised, Stuffed Flank Steak

(3 TO 4 SERVINGS)

Mrs. Aldo Nerelli, Pesenti Winery, Templeton
Editor's note: Dry red wine both flavors and tenderizes this stuffed flank steak

1 to 1½ pound flank steak
¼ cup minced onion
1 tablespoon butter
2 cups fresh bread crumbs
1 tablespoon snipped parsley
½ teaspoon salt
⅛ teaspoon pepper
½ teaspoon celery salt
½ teaspoon dried sage
2 tablespoons butter
1 tablespoon fat or oil
½ cup California
   Red Table Wine
½ cup hot water
½ teaspoon peppercorns
1 teaspoon garlic wine vinegar
   GRAVY
½ cup California
   Red Table Wine
½ cup water
1 beef bouillon cube
¼ cup flour
6 tablespoons cold water

Have butcher score one side of steak in diamond pattern. Sauté onions in butter. Add crumbs, parsley and seasonings. Add warm water to make stuffing of desired consistency. Arrange on unscored side of steak, patting it until it nearly reaches the edges. Dot with butter. Roll up loosely, jelly-roll fashion; secure with skewers or string, leaving room for expansion of stuffing. In hot fat in Dutch oven, brown steak well on both sides—about 15 minutes. Add wine and water, peppercorns and sprinkle with vinegar. Simmer, tightly covered or bake in oven 350° for 1½ hours or until tender. Place meat on platter, remove string and slice. **Gravy:** Strain the liquid in which meat was cooked. To it add wine, water and bouillon cube. Mix flour with cold water and stir into wine and broth mixture. Heat, stirring until gravy is hot and thickened.

Editor's note: With this dish, serve the California Red Table Wine used in preparing it. **CALIFORNIA BURGUNDY** *or* **CABERNET** *is a good choice.*

Steaks Dianne

(10 TO 12 SERVINGS)

Mrs. Kay Martin, California Growers Winery, Cutler
I use an electric griddle and cook at the table at 375°, usually in two or three batches, using proportionate amounts of butter and sauce for each cooking. Green salad and a green bean or zucchini casserole make this meal complete. Pilaf is also a good accompaniment.

Steak buns
1 beef tenderloin
   sliced in ¼ inch slices
½ cup butter
1 cup California Burgundy
1 teaspoon salt
¼ teaspoon freshly ground
   pepper
1 clove garlic, minced
1 tablespoon chopped parsley

Have buns hot and the rest of the dinner ready to serve before cooking the steaks. Cook the steaks quickly in butter, then pour over them the rest of the ingredients and heat through. Serve two steaks on each bun. Spoon some of the heated sauce over the meat.

My choice of wine to accompany this dish:
CALIFORNIA SPARKLING BURGUNDY

International Angus Steak

(6 SERVINGS)

Mrs. William Perelli-Minetti, A. Perelli-Minetti & Sons, Delano
Editor's note: This way of cooking cube steaks is well named. It starts off in an oriental manner, but the Bulgur wheat (instead of the rice one would expect) gives it a middle European flavor.

6 cube steaks
¼ cup soy sauce
   Flour
   Salt, pepper
¼ cup cooking oil
½ cup chopped onion
½ cup chopped green pepper
⅔ cup bulgur wheat
4 teaspoons cornstarch
1 cup California Burgundy
½ cup water
2 tablespoon chopped parsley

Cut the cube steaks into strips 2″ long by 1″ wide. Sprinkle soy sauce on each side. Roll the strips in flour, then season with salt and pepper. Brown steak in a large electric frypan in hot cooking oil. When partly brown add onion and green pepper; sauté until barely tender. Cover browned ingredients with bulgur. Blend cornstarch, wine and water; add to ingredients in pan. Sprinkle parsley on top. Simmer about 30 minutes at low temperature until wheat is done. A little more wine or water may be added to keep it from getting too dry.

 Editor's note: Try a **CALIFORNIA BURGUNDY** *or* **GAMAY** *with this dish.*

Korean Steaks

(12 TO 15 SERVINGS)

Mrs. Kay Martin, California Growers Wineries, Cutler
These steaks are the specialty of Korean friends of ours. We have substituted wine for half of the soy sauce they used. With the steaks we serve plain boiled rice (using the marinade as a sauce) or a pilaf, green salad and hot buttered French bread. We have fresh fruit for dessert as this is usually prepared in the summer barbecue season. Otherwise, sherbet is good.

1 (5 to 6-lb.) standing rib roast
1 package sesame seeds
1 cup soy sauce
1 cup California Burgundy
½ cup oil
2 cloves garlic, minced
1 bunch green onions, minced, including part of the tops
½ green pepper, minced
1 teaspoon monosodium glutamate
1 teaspoon freshly ground pepper
1 tablespoon sugar

Have butcher bone roast and remove part of the fat, then cut in 3/16-inch slices. (My butcher uses the slicing machine and gets about 5 steaks per pound.) Toast the sesame seeds in a dry frying pan, stirring constantly until they are a light brown. Put them between two sheets of waxed paper and crush thoroughly with a rolling pin. Mix with all other ingredients to make marinade. Put a layer of steaks in a shallow dish and cover with marinade, being sure to get some of the solids on each steak. Add another layer of steaks with marinade until all steaks and marinade are used. Marinate at least six hours, turning the steaks over occasionally so the liquid can be kept distributed. Cook steaks over a hot barbecue fire. Cook on first side until brown shows through (only a few minutes), then flip and cook on other side briefly. These cook so fast that it is a good idea to have your guests already seated and served with their other food before you start the cooking process. Most guests will eat two of these steaks.

My choice of wine to accompany this dish: **CALIFORNIA BURGUNDY** *or on especially festive occasions* **SPARKLING BURGUNDY**

Beef Burgundy

(6 SERVINGS)

Mrs. Arthur Caputi, Jr., E. & J. Gallo Winery, Modesto
Re-heating even improves the flavor of this already rich dish. So this is a perfect make-ahead company recipe. Favorite accompaniments are Caesar salad, French bread, and lemon sherbet with raspberry sauce.

¼ cup butter
2½ pounds boneless stew meat, cut into 1-inch cubes
½ lb. small white onions, peeled
½ lb. small fresh mushrooms
4 tablespoon flour
2½ teaspoons beef stock base
2 tablespoons tomato paste
1½ cups California Burgundy
¾ cup California Dry Sherry
¾ cup California Ruby Port
2 tablespoons California Brandy
1 (10½-oz.) can condensed beef bouillon, undiluted
⅛ teaspoon pepper
1 bay leaf

Melt half the butter in 4-quart Dutch oven and brown beef cubes well all over. Lift out beef as it browns. Add remaining butter to Dutch oven and add onions; cook over low heat, covered, until slightly browned. Add mushrooms and cook for about 3 minutes. Remove from heat and add flour, beef stock base and tomato paste. Stir until well blended. Stir in wines, Brandy and beef bouillon. Bring wine mixture just to boiling, stirring, remove from heat and add beef, pepper and bay leaf. Bake in 350° oven, covered, for approximately 1½ hours.

My choice of wine to accompany this dish:
CALIFORNIA BURGUNDY *or* **CABERNET SAUVIGNON**

Napa Valley Meat Roll

(4 SERVINGS)

Mrs. William Bonetti, Charles Krug Winery, St. Helena
This dish can be made a day in advance and reheated very slowly before serving.

1 (2-lb.) piece round steak (about ½ inch thick)
Salt, pepper
2 onions, sliced
¼ pound mushrooms
1 green pepper, sliced
3 tablespoons butter
1½ cups fine, dry bread crumbs
1 (2-oz.) jar stuffed olives, drained and sliced
Flour
2 tablespoons butter
6 tablespoons olive oil
Few leaves of sage, rosemary, oregano and a sprig of parsley
2 cups California Burgundy

Pound steak until thin; rub in salt and pepper. Sauté onions, mushrooms, and green pepper with 3 tablespoons butter and spread it on steak; cover with bread crumbs; blanket with a layer of sliced olives. Roll meat and tie roll firmly. Flour outside. Brown in butter and olive oil. Add herbs. Add wine, bring to boil, then cover and simmer about 3 hours.

My choice of wine to accompany this dish:
CALIFORNIA ZINFANDEL *or* **GAMAY**

18

Steak Bordelaise, Vermouth

(6 TO 8 SERVINGS)

Miss Helen V. Reynolds, United Vintners, San Francisco
This recipe has been a long-time favorite with the Eyrud family in Paris and is
usually served at family gatherings.

6 to 8 medium size
   tenderloin tips
   (or tender top round)
Salt and pepper
⅓ cup sifted flour
¼ cup olive oil
1 (4 to 6-oz.) can mushrooms,
   sliced, or ½ pound fresh
   button mushrooms, sliced
2 cloves garlic, finely chopped
¼ cup finely chopped parsley
½ cup California Dry Vermouth
¼ cup olive oil

Roll tenderloin tips in seasoned flour, and brown in olive oil. Add mushrooms, chopped garlic, parsley and liquid from mushrooms (if canned mushrooms are used). Add Vermouth, cover and simmer over low heat for 10 to 15 minutes, or until liquid has cooked down.

Note: If there is not enough liquid after Vermouth and water from mushrooms have been added, a small amount of Burgundy may also be added. The idea is to have enough liquid for the garlic and parsley to cook in.

My choice of wine to accompany this dish:
CALIFORNIA VIN ROSÉ *or* **PINOT NOIR**

Entrecote with Watercress

(6 SERVINGS)

Mrs. Janet Schultz, Fromm and Sichel, San Francisco
Editor's note: Good steaks deserve a good wine sauce. This one is easy and excellent.

Olive oil
2 sirloin steaks,
   large enough for 6 persons
Salt and pepper
2 tablespoons chopped shallots
1 tablespoon butter
¾ cup California Sauterne
3 tablespoons chopped parsley
Watercress

Barely cover the bottoms of 2 large frying pans with olive oil and heat. Trim most of the fat from the steaks. Season with salt and pepper. Cook in hot oil, 5 minutes on each side. Remove steaks to hot platter. Meanwhile, in small saucepan brown shallots in butter. Add wine and parsley. Cook, stirring occasionally, until wine is reduced by half. Serve steaks topped with shallots and wine sauce and surrounded with watercress.

Editor's note: A worthy wine accompaniment is either a
CALIFORNIA BURGUNDY *or* **CABERNET SAUVIGNON.**

Wine Short Ribs

(5 TO 6 SERVINGS)

Mrs. Kenneth Huff, Wine Institute, San Francisco
Editor's note: The tartness of the red table wine along with the acid of the wine vinegar
improve the flavor and cut the richness of these braised short ribs.

2 pounds lean short ribs
Salt and pepper
Flour
3 tablespoons bacon fat
   or cooking oil
½ cup California
   Red Table Wine
3 tablespoons catsup
2 tablespoons California
   red wine vinegar
1 tablespoon minced onion

Season short ribs with salt and pepper and dust with flour. In a heavy roasting pan, heat fat or oil and brown meat thoroughly. Discard any excess fat. Meanwhile, combine remaining ingredients. Pour over meat. Cover and bake in 375° oven for 1¼ to 1½ hours until meat is tender. Baste with the wine sauce during the baking period.

 My choice of wine to accompany this dish: **CALIFORNIA BURGUNDY**

Flaming Beef Grenadine

(6 SERVINGS)

Mrs. Jack Matthews, Wine Institute, San Francisco

6 slices fillet of beef tenderloin
⅓ cup butter
6 shallots, chopped
¾ pound fresh mushrooms,
    sliced
⅔ cup California Port
⅔ cup California Brandy
Dash each: salt, pepper,
    monosodium glutamate
Dash Worcestershire sauce

Sauté fillets in butter until browned well on both sides; add and brown shallots and mushrooms; add Port. Add Brandy (at table if you want maximum eye appeal) ignite and let flame burn out. Add seasonings.

My choice of wine to accompany this dish:
CALIFORNIA CABERNET SAUVIGNON

Boeuf à la Bourguignonne

(6 GENEROUS SERVINGS)

Harry G. Serlis, Wine Institute, San Francisco
Editor's note: This takes two days, but it's worth the time. It has superb flavor and appearance.

5 lbs. round or chuck steak
    cut into large cubes
    (approx. 2½ x 2½ x 2″)
    Flour
5 tablespoons olive oil
¼ cup butter
    Salt, pepper
½ cup warm California Brandy
½ lb. bacon, cut up
2 cloves garlic, minced
2 carrots, minced
2 leeks, chopped
6 scallions or green onions,
    chopped
2 medium onions, chopped
1 lb. mushrooms
1 lamb shank, split
    (or calves foot)
½ teaspoon dried thyme
2 bay leaves
1 stalk celery and leaves
4 sprigs parsley
1 fifth bottle
    California Burgundy
    Water
2 tablespoons flour
1 tablespoon kitchen bouquet
1 tablespoon butter
6 small onions, peeled
    Sugar
1 tablespoon butter
1 tablespoon olive oil
    Lemon juice
    Chopped parsley

Roll cubes of beef in flour. Heat 5 tablespoons oil and half of the butter in a large skillet over a high heat and brown the meat well on all sides. Sprinkle the meat with salt and pepper, pour Brandy over it, ignite and let flame die out. Transfer contents of skillet to a large oven-proof casserole or Dutch oven (preferably clay). Sauté the diced bacon in the skillet until crisp and brown. Add garlic, carrots, leeks, scallions, onions and chopped mushroom stems. Save mushroom caps. Cook, stirring occasionally until all the vegetables are lightly browned. Transfer vegetables to the casserole with the meat. Add to the casserole the lamb shank, and the thyme and bay leaf, celery stalk and some of the parsley tied into a bouquet garni. (You can leave the lamb shank loose if you wish. However, later you will have to remove the bones and gristle from the stew. Do this if you would like the meat from the lamb shank in the stew.) Add all but one cup of the wine and add enough water to cover contents. Cover and bake in 350° oven for 2 hours. (Let stand overnight in refrigerator.) Next morning remove fat from the top of the stew. Stir in flour mixed into a paste with water or some melted butter, stir in kitchen bouquet and continue to bake at 350° for another 2 or 3 hours. Just before serving, melt 1 tablespoon butter in a saucepan; add the small onions, sprinkle with a little sugar, cook stirring until onions are browned, add a little of the remaining wine. Cover and simmer for 20 minutes. In a skillet heat the remaining 1 tablespoon butter and the 1 tablespoon olive oil and in it place the mushrooms, cap side down. Sprinkle with lemon juice and sauté mushrooms for 2 minutes longer. Add a little wine to the skillet and keep mushrooms warm. When ready to serve, remove excess fat, again, from the top of the liquid. Discard calf's foot (or lamb shank) and the bouquet garni. Stir in the remaining wine, thicken gravy if desired, adjust seasonings and arrange onions and mushrooms around the meat and garnish with parsley.

My choice of wine to accompany this dish: A robust red table wine such as
CALIFORNIA CLARET *or* CABERNET SAUVIGNON

Sweetbreads Vermouth

(6 SERVINGS)

Mrs. B. C. Solari, United Vintners, San Francisco
We call this a Sunday brunch dish. Sometimes we serve it with scrambled eggs and sometimes we surround the sweetbreads with crisp bacon, link sausages or broiled slices of ham.
Fresh fruit or juice starts the brunch. Toasted, buttered French bread completes the menu.

2 pounds sweetbreads
⅓ cup butter
½ pound sliced mushrooms
 Salt, pepper
½ cup California Dry Vermouth
½ teaspoon fresh, broken
  sage leaves
 Chopped parsley
 Grated lemon peel

Prepare sweetbreads in the usual manner, soaking in cold water briefly, then blanching in boiling water for 10 to 20 minutes. Cool. Remove all fat and membranes, and cut into one or 1½-inch cubes. Melt butter. When bubbling slowly, add sweetbreads. Cook, turning frequently, until golden brown. Add mushrooms (I prefer these also blanched for about 5 minutes) and cook about 10 minutes. Stir in seasonings, Vermouth and sprinkle with sage. Simmer 10 or 15 minutes more. Remove to heated platter and sprinkle with parsley and lemon peel.

My choice of wine to accompany this dish:
CALIFORNIA CHENIN BLANC *or* **JOHANNISBERG RIESLING**

La Lunga

(6 TO 8 SERVINGS)

Miss Jacqueline Guimina, The Christian Brothers, Reedley
Editor's note: A dry white wine gives beef tongue such an excellent flavor, it's good hot or cold.
Serve gravy separately if some of the tongue is to be reserved for a second meal.

1 large beef tongue
  (3 to 4 pounds)
2 medium onions
3 tablespoons butter
¼ cup chopped parsley
1 teaspoon Italian seasoning
½ teaspoon salt
⅛ teaspoon pepper
½ pound fresh mushrooms,
  sliced
4 tablespoons flour
1 (13¾-oz.) can chicken broth
1 teaspoon beef extract
¾ cup California Dry Sauterne

Cover tongue with cold water. Add one chopped onion and salt. Bring to boil and simmer for approximately 2½ hours, or until tender. Sauté one minced onion in butter; add chopped parsley, seasonings, and mushrooms. Cook for 5 minutes while slowly adding flour and 2 cups of broth from tongue. Add chicken broth, beef extract and wine; simmer for 30 minutes. Skin tongue while hot and slice on a platter. Pour the hot gravy over tongue slices and garnish with parsley.

My choice of wine to accompany this dish:
A hearty **CALIFORNIA RED WINE**
Editor's note: **CALIFORNIA BURGUNDY, PINOT ST. GEORGE** *or* **CABERNET SAUVIGNON** *are especially suitable.*

Ernie's Tenderloin Brochette with Bordelaise Sauce

(4 SERVINGS)

Mrs. George Al Berry, E. & J. Gallo Winery, Modesto
I am indebted to my good friend, Paul Quiarud, the chef at Ernie's restaurant in San Francisco,
for this recipe. To complete the menu I serve Vischyssoise, then a crisp lettuce salad with
Gourmet Dressing (Page 68). With the beef, I serve a risotto of wild rice and for dessert,
Strawberries Romanoff.

2 **pounds tenderloin of beef**
2 **green peppers**
4 **slices bacon**
16 **whole mushrooms**
Salt and pepper
Olive oil

BORDELAISE SAUCE
1 **stalk celery**
½ **small carrot**
½ **small onion, chopped**
2 **cloves garlic, minced**
¼ **cup butter**
1 **teaspoon pickling spice**
Pinch of rosemary
½ **cup tomato puree**
½ **cup strong beef stock**
    (or canned beef bouillon)
½ **cup California**
    Red Table Wine
Juice of 1 lemon
Pinch of nutmeg
2 **egg yolks, well beaten**
Salt and pepper
¼ **cup melted butter**
Chopped parsley

Cut beef into 16 pieces, each about one inch thick. Parboil green peppers in boiling water; drain, cool and cut into 16 squares. Cut each bacon slice into 4 pieces. Using four 10-inch skewers, first spear a piece of meat, then a square of green pepper, then bacon, then a mushroom. Repeat until each skewer contains 4 pieces of meat. Sprinkle with salt and pepper and roll in olive oil, then put on rack of preheated broiler. Broil two minutes for medium-rare or 1½ minutes for rare. Serve with Bordelaise Sauce and wild rice. **Bordelaise Sauce:** Cut celery and carrot in one-half inch lengths. Add onions and garlic and sauté in butter. Add pickling spice and rosemary and cook until vegetables are well browned. Then add tomato puree, beef stock, wine, lemon juice, and nutmeg. Boil and reduce to half its volume. Strain and discard vegetables and spices. Add strained sauce to well-beaten yolks, beating constantly until thoroughly mixed and slightly thickened. Adjust seasoning. Keep hot, but do not allow to boil. Just before serving, beat in melted butter and parsley.

My choice of wine to accompany this dish:
A **CALIFORNIA RIESLING** *or* **CHABLIS** *is good with first two courses,
and* **CALIFORNIA PINOT NOIR** *with the main course.*

Wild Boar Larkmead

(10 SERVINGS)

Mr. B. C. Solari, United Vintners, San Francisco
This is a rare taste treat. We get the wild boar from Mr. Stuyvesant Fish
of Palo Corona Ranch in Carmel, California.

2 **Haunches of a 35 to 40 pound**
    wild boar
Garlic
Rosemary
Salt and pepper
Olive oil
1 **(7½-oz.) can unpitted**
    black olives
1½ **cups California**
    Dry White Wine

Cut boar like leg of lamb. Cut several slits in meat and insert small pieces of garlic, several needles of rosemary, salt and pepper in the little pockets (3 or 4 to the haunch). Place haunches on large flat baking pan. Pour olive oil over all leaving about ⅛ inch depth in pan. Put in very hot oven (500°) until brown for 15 or 20 minutes. Lower oven to 400° and cook 45 minutes or longer, until done. During last 20 minutes, add 1 can of black olives, with pits, and add wine.

My choice of wine to accompany this dish:
CALIFORNIA CABERNET SAUVIGNON *or* **CHARBONO**

Kidneys Hunter Style

(6 SERVINGS)

Mrs. Philip G. Smyser, Wine Advisory Board, San Francisco
This is excellent for a party breakfast or brunch with omelets. It makes a good dinner dish also.

6 veal or 12 lamb kidneys
½ cup butter
1 teaspoon chopped parsley
1 teaspoon onion (or chives)
1½ tablespoons flour
½ cup each California
    Madeira, dry white wine,
    chicken broth
½ pound mushrooms,
    thinly sliced
¼ cup butter

Plunge kidneys into boiling water, drain them immediately, and remove the thin skins and tough centers. Cut kidneys into thin slices. Sauté slices in ½ cup butter, until lightly browned. Add parsley and onion and cook mixture over high heat for 2 minutes. Sprinkle with flour and blend well. Add wines and broth and bring to a boil, reduce heat and simmer, stirring constantly, for 5 minutes. Sauté mushrooms in ¼ cup butter until soft. Add them to kidneys and cook whole mixture for another 3 minutes. Serve garnished with parsley on toasted English muffins.

 My choice of wine to accompany this dish: **CALIFORNIA CHAMPAGNE**

Beef Heart Pinot Blanc

(4 TO 6 SERVINGS)

Mrs. N. C. Mirassou, Mirassou Vineyards, San Jose
Editor's note: Dry white wine and more-than-a-little garlic give beef heart plenty of flavor.
After long simmering, it is finished off with Brandy.

3 to 4 pounds beef heart
1 bottle California Pinot Blanc
    Salt, pepper, monosodium
        glutamate
¾ cup parsley,
    chopped very fine
½ cup chives
5 ·or 6 small cloves garlic,
    chopped very fine
15 large button mushrooms,
    sliced into 3 parts
⅓ cup California Brandy

Wash heart and cut into ½-inch strips. Use electric fry pan, set at 300°. Put 2 cups wine in fry pan, then add heart, salt, pepper and monosodium glutamate. Cook for 25 minutes before turning. After turning, add parsley, chives, garlic and mushrooms. Add more wine as needed. Cover and simmer until tender (about 2 hours). Just before done add California Brandy.

 My choice of wine to accompany this dish: **CALIFORNIA PINOT BLANC**

Puchero Chollo

(6 TO 8 SERVINGS)

Mr. and Mrs. Ferrer Filipello, Italian Swiss Colony, Asti
Editor's note: Meat and vegetables are cooked together for a hearty one-dish meal. The stock makes an excellent first course for this or another meal. Asked what they like to serve to complete the menu, the contributors said, "serve with some sour dough French bread."

4 quarts water
1 teaspoon salt
⅛ teaspoon monosodium
    glutamate
⅛ teaspoon black pepper
2 pounds beef short ribs
½ pound lean salt pork, sliced
1 chicken, disjointed
3 chorizo (Spanish sausage)
6 peeled carrots
2 cups canned garbanzo
    (chick peas) No. 303 can,
    drained
6 medium onions
6 small cloves garlic, minced
1 zucchini squash, sliced
6 tomatoes
1 head cabbage, cut in eighths
1 green pepper, chopped
6 peeled potatoes
6 green onions
2 tablespoons chopped parsley
1 cup California Dry Sherry

Bring to a slow boil 4 quarts water. Add salt, monosodium glutamate, pepper, beef, pork, chicken and simmer for 1½ hours. Add chorizo and carrots. Simmer 30 minutes. Add all other vegetables and cook until potatoes are tender. Add Sherry. Arrange meat on platter, surround with vegetables. Serve stock as soup.

Our choice of wine to accompany this dish:
CALIFORNIA DRY SHERRY *with the soup,*
CALIFORNIA CLARET *with the meat.*

Veal Scallops, Roman Style

(6 SERVINGS)

Mrs. George Pentek, The Christian Brothers, Fresno
Editor's note: The sage and white wine are traditional seasonings for veal in this recipe of Italian ancestry.

6 thin serving-size pieces veal
    round (about 1½ pounds)
    Salt, pepper, powdered sage
6 wafer-thin slices prosciutto,
    ham or Canadian bacon
3 tablespoons butter
¼ cup California
    White Table Wine
6 thin slices natural Swiss
    or mozzarella cheese

Pound pieces of veal steak with mallet to make as thin as possible. Sprinkle lightly with salt, pepper and powdered sage, or use a leaf of fresh sage. Cover each piece with prosciutto or ham. Pin into place with picks, or roll and tie with string. Cook gently in butter over moderate heat until golden brown on all sides, a total of 6 to 8 minutes (overcooking toughens and dries out veal). Place on heatproof platter; keep hot. Add wine to pan; scrape up bottom. Heat until bubbly and pour over veal. For extra embellishment, before adding pan sauce, top each serving with a slice of cheese. Run under broiler to glaze.

My choice of wine to accompany this dish: **CALIFORNIA VIN ROSÉ**

Loin of Pork, Larkmead

(6 SERVINGS)

B. C. Solari, United Vintners, Inc., San Francisco
This pork roast is cooked in a covered barbecue oven, but can also be done on a rotating grill, if it is basted frequently. Our menu in summer for a distinguished luncheon when guests are males with hearty appetites: cold Vichyssoise or hot chicken broth with a slice of lemon; the roast, presliced and served on a platter garnished with parsley; sauce in a separate bowl; fresh applesauce; asparagus with hollandaise sauce; green salad with oil and wine vinegar dressing. For dessert, fresh fruit, assorted cheese, French bread.

1　12-rib pork loin
1　cup soy sauce
2　tablespoons Worcestershire sauce
1　cup honey (or maple syrup)
1　cup California Red Table Wine
¼　cup dry mustard
1　cup wine vinegar
　　Salt and pepper

Have butcher remove bone from pork loin, then tie bone to the meat to add flavor during cooking. Prepare marinade by combining all remaining ingredients in blender and mixing thoroughly. Marinate pork in a large flat baking dish for 4 or 5 hours. Turn occasionally. In covered barbecue oven, build a slow fire of coals. Place aluminum foil in an old pan on grate. Set roast on foil. Baste generously and often with marinade. Cook, covered, 1½ hours. During last 15 minutes, heat remaining marinade until it thickens slightly. Serve as sauce for meat.

My choice of wine to accompany this dish:
CALIFORNIA PINOT NOIR *or* **PINOT CHARDONNAY**

Cream Sherry Porkchops

(4 SERVINGS)

Mrs. Richard Nagoaka, The Christian Brothers, Napa
Editor's note: Both the sweetness and the caramel flavor of Cream Sherry enhance porkchops simmered and served in a creamy sauce. To take best advantage of the sauce, serve this dish with rice or noodles. Round out the meal with brussels sprouts, orange and grapefruit sections tossed with salad greens, and Apple-Brandy Cake (Page 88) for dessert.

　　Flour
　　Salt and pepper
1　teaspoon sage, crumbled or powdered
4　porkchops (about 1½ pounds)
¼　cup onions, diced
1　(10½-oz.) can cream of mushroom soup
½　cup milk or water
¾　cup California Cream Sherry
½　cup sliced mushrooms
1　cup dairy sour cream

Flour and season porkchops. Brown porkchops and add onions. Combine mushroom soup, milk, and Sherry. Pour sauce over porkchops. Add sliced mushrooms. Cover and simmer 45 to 50 minutes or until tender, stirring occasionally. Add the sour cream 2 minutes before serving. When the gravy is at preferred consistency, serve with steamed white rice. If the gravy becomes too thick, add more milk.

My choice of wine to accompany this dish:
CALIFORNIA GAMAY, CHABLIS *or* **PINOT CHARDONNAY**

Mib's Lamb Shanks

(6 SERVINGS)

Mrs. John G. Laucci, Franzia Brothers Winery, Ripon
These lamb shanks seem to call for curried rice. We usually add a tossed green salad with olive
oil and wine vinegar dressing, and serve cheesecake or lemon pie for dessert.

6 **lamb shanks**
1½ **teaspoons salt**
1 **teaspoon pepper**
1 **teaspoon powdered oregano**
1½ **teaspoons sweet basil**
1 **tablespoon monosodium glutamate**
1 **large clove garlic**
1½ **tablespoons fresh or dry rosemary**
¼ **cup olive oil**
3 **tablespoons wine vinegar**
½ **cup water**
½ **cup California Sauterne or Chablis**
½ **cup olive oil**
1 **cup flour**
1 **large red onion, sliced thin**
6 to 8 **red potatoes, quartered**
6 to 8 **pieces dry mushrooms soaked in water then chopped or ½ pound fresh mushrooms, sliced**
½ **cup water**
¾ **cup California Sauterne or Chablis**
1 **(10-oz.) package frozen carrots**
1 **(10-oz.) package frozen peas**

Place lamb shanks in deep platter or large bowl in single layer, if possible. Pour over a marinade made by combining salt, pepper, oregano, basil, monosodium glutamate, garlic, rosemary, ¼ cup olive oil, wine vinegar, ½ cup water and ½ cup wine. Allow to stand at least 1 hour, turning several times. In a large, heavy skillet, heat ½ cup olive oil. Flour shanks and cook in oil over medium heat until they are brown on all sides, about 20 minutes. Pour off all fat drippings. Add mushrooms, onions, potatoes, ½ cup water and ¾ cup wine. Allow to simmer over low heat for about 2½ hours. Add more wine and water if necessary. About 20 minutes before shanks are ready, add frozen carrots and peas. Stir gently. To serve: Place cooked curried rice on plate with shank in center. Spoon vegetables and juice around shank. Top with 1 sprinkling of fresh parsley.

 My choice of wine to accompany this dish: **CALIFORNIA CHABLIS**

Baked Ham Steak

(6 TO 8 SERVINGS)

Mrs. Jon B. Shastid, E. & J. Gallo Winery, Modesto
Editor's note: Ham steak is moist and flavorful when cooked in this way with a mixture of
wine and milk. Made with these proportions, the sauce has a definite mustard flavor—
complementary to the meat.

1 **center slice of ham (about 2 inches thick)**
1 **cup milk**
1 **cup California Rhine Wine or other white table wine**
Prepared mustard

Place slice of ham in deep baking dish (8 x 12 x 2 inches is a good size). Pour over ham first milk then wine. Liquid should barely cover ham and come about half inch from top of dish. Bake in moderate oven (350°) for about one hour, turning ham steak over after 30 minutes baking. To make sauce, measure drippings in pan and add one-third as much prepared mustard.

Editor's note: Either **CALIFORNIA RIESLING** *or* **ROSÉ** *goes very well with this dish.*

Spanish Lamb

(6 TO 8 SERVINGS)

Mrs. Paul J. Lunardi, Wine Institute, San Francisco
Editor's note: Adding the wine at the end of the simmering period will preserve the wine flavor in the finished dish. Whenever wine is added earlier in the cooking period, it blends with the other seasonings and is not usually identifiable.

5 strips bacon, cut fine
4 cups boneless lamb shoulder,
    cut in 1-inch cubes
    (3 pounds)
⅓ cup flour
    Salt, pepper
1½ cups sliced peeled onions
3 cups diced celery
¾ teaspoon powdered sugar
1½ tablespoons lemon juice
3 cups tomato juice, canned or
    strained canned tomatoes
1½ teaspoons Worcestershire
    sauce
1½ teaspoons salt
⅛ teaspoon pepper
½ cup California
    Red Table Wine
3 cups green peas, uncooked

In a deep skillet or Dutch oven, cook bacon until light brown, about 5 minutes. Sprinkle lamb with flour, salt and pepper. Brown in bacon fat along with onions. Add remaining ingredients, except wine and peas, bring to a boil, then simmer 1 hour or until tender. Add wine and peas about 10 minutes before it is completely done.

 My choice of wine to accompany this dish:
CALIFORNIA CABERNET SAUVIGNON

Roasted Lamb Shanks with Potatoes

(4 TO 6 SERVINGS)

Mrs. Michael Filice, San Martin Vineyards, San Martin
This recipe originated in Calabria, Italy, and was handed down many generations in our family. Lamb is a favorite meat, especially at Easter. There always was a shaker of red hot pepper on the table, and the old timers would sprinkle their roast generously with it.

4 lamb shanks (about 3 pounds)
1 large clove garlic
2 teaspoons salt
    Oregano
    Monosodium glutamate
    Pepper
1 cup California Sauterne
3 tablespoons lemon juice
    Pinch chopped fresh
    rosemary
4 to 6 medium potatoes

Have butcher cut bone in 3 places. Wash shanks and place in large shallow pan. Place bits of garlic between cut bone and press together. Sprinkle with salt, oregano, monosodium glutamate and pepper. Bake in 450° oven. Mix wine, lemon juice and rosemary. As meat browns baste with wine mixture. Brown slowly and well on all sides, about ¾ hour. Then add a little of the wine mixture to bottom of pan. Cover with foil, and bake 350° for about 45 minutes. During this time prepare 4 to 6 medium potatoes, season and add alongside shanks. If pan is dry, add a little more wine or water, cover and bake until potatoes are tender, about 45 minutes.

 My choice of wine to accompany this dish: **CALIFORNIA BURGUNDY**

27

Sherried Lamb in Patty Shells

(6 SERVINGS)

Mrs. George Al Berry, E. & J. Gallo Winery, Modesto
I usually serve this recipe as a luncheon dish, preceded by cold consomme and accompanied by a grapefruit-cucumber molded salad and hot rolls. If dessert is served, it should be on the light side. I usually choose fresh fruit in season, such as strawberries or melons, or if none is available, ice cream or sherbet.

1   (10-oz.) package
       frozen patty shells
¼   cup sliced green onions
¼   lb. mushrooms, sliced
¼   cup butter or margarine
¼   cup flour
1   teaspoon salt
¼   teaspoon rosemary leaves
⅛   teaspoon pepper
½   cup milk
1   cup light cream
2   cups diced, cooked lamb
2   tablespoons diced
       canned pimiento
¼   cup California Dry Sherry

Prepare frozen patty shells according to directions on package. Sauté onions and mushrooms in butter until tender. Stir in flour and seasonings. Gradually add milk and cream; cook, stirring constantly until sauce thickens and boils. Add lamb, pimiento, and Sherry; mix and heat thoroughly. Spoon into hot patty shells on serving plate.

🍷 *My choice of wine to accompany this dish:*
CALIFORNIA GREY RIESLING *or* **CHABLIS**

Rabbit à la Borghese

(5 TO 6 SERVINGS)

Mrs. Armand E. Bussone, Almaden Vineyards, Los Gatos
This is a northern Italian recipe brought to America by my mother-in-law. When she originally gave it to me, the recipe contained terms such as "a handful of this and a pinch of that." After years of experimentation, I feel these measurements are equivalent to the original quaint ones. This recipe can be prepared a day in advance because it tastes even better after being refrigerated 24 hours. It goes well with baked potatoes (mashed, whipped and replaced in skins) and a tossed salad plus any other favorite vegetable.

1   (2½-lb.) rabbit, cut up
3   tablespoons oil
½   medium red onion,
       finely chopped
¼   cup parsley, finely chopped
2   tablespoons butter
¼   cup California Chablis
       Juice of ½ lemon
1   teaspoon flour
1   (10½-oz.) can consomme
    Salt and pepper

Brown the rabbit in oil. In another skillet, slowly sauté onion and parsley in butter. Add rabbit. In the original browning pan, combine wine, lemon juice, and the flour mixed with water to form a paste so that it will blend smoothly with the other liquids. Simmer for three minutes. Add this to rabbit mixture. Finally, add the consommé and enough water to cover rabbit. Season with salt and pepper. Cover and cook slowly for 1 hour and 20 minutes. Note: If you're looking for a new tasty chicken dish, simply substitute a chicken for the rabbit in the above recipe and change the name to Chicken a la Borghese.

🍷 *My choice of wine to accompany this dish:* **CALIFORNIA RIESLING**

Veal Vermouth

(4 SERVINGS)

Mrs. Herbert L. Grosswendt, Brookside Vineyard Company, Agoura
I love this company recipe because it can all be prepared ahead of time. A little extra time on the stove won't hurt the flavor either. Finding this recipe in a magazine many years ago changed my cooking reputation overnight from "Bridal" to "Gourmet."

1½ **pounds veal cutlet**
1 **clove garlic**
Flour
¼ **cup margarine**
½ **pound fresh mushrooms, thinly sliced**
½ **teaspoon salt**
Pepper
⅓ **cup California Dry Vermouth**
1 **teaspoon lemon juice**
¼ **cup snipped parsley**

Wheedle the butcher into cutting your veal into very thin slices, then pound them even thinner. Rub veal all over with cut garlic clove and dip slices in flour. Heat margarine and add veal, several slices at a time, until they're golden brown on each side. Heap mushrooms on meat; sprinkle with salt, dash pepper and Vermouth. Cover and simmer 20 minutes or until fork tender. Just before serving, sprinkle lemon juice and parsley over all.

 My choice of wine to accompany this dish: **CALIFORNIA VIN ROSÉ**

Veal Steaks, Sauterne

(6 SERVINGS)

Miss Diana Weibel, Weibel Champagne Vineyards, Mission San Jose
Editor's note: These breaded veal steaks are well-seasoned and exceptionally tender, thanks to the wine and tomato sauce in which they are simmered.

1 **onion, finely chopped**
1 **green pepper, finely chopped**
3 **tablespoons butter**
2 **tomatoes, sliced**
10 **mushrooms, sliced**
2 **(8-oz.) cans tomato sauce**
1 **teaspoon sweet basil**
1 **teaspoon oregano**
1 **teaspoon salt**
½ **teaspoon pepper**
6 **veal steaks**
1 **egg, well beaten**
Fine, dry bread crumbs
Cooking oil
½ **cup grated Parmesan cheese**
1 **cup California Sauterne**
Juice of 1 lemon
6 **slices mozzarella cheese**

Sauté onion and green pepper in butter until golden brown. Then add tomatoes, mushrooms, tomato sauce and seasonings. Simmer while preparing meat. Dip veal steaks in egg, then in bread crumbs. Fry in oil until golden brown. Place in a casserole and pour tomato mixture over meat. Sprinkle Parmesan cheese over top. Pour on wine and lemon juice. Cover and bake in slow oven, 325° for 45 minutes or until tender. Just before serving, place a slice of mozzarella cheese on top of each steak and broil until cheese melts.

 Editor's note: Either a **CALIFORNIA PINOT CHARDONNAY** *or* **ROSÉ** *would be a perfect complement to this dish.*

Veal Sauté

(18 SERVINGS)

Mrs. Frank Franzia, Sr., Franzia Brothers Winery, Ripon
This is our favorite recipe. We have used it many times for dinner parties—buffet style.
Editor's note: It's too good to be reserved only for company. Cut it in half or thirds for an
excellent family meal. Serve it with rice or noodles, peas or other green vegetable, and a
salad of mixed greens with a sharp wine vinegar and olive oil dressing.

8 pounds veal stew meat,
    cut in 1½-inch cubes
4 teaspoons salt
½ teaspoon pepper
¼ cup salad oil
2 (4-oz.) cans sliced
    mushrooms, drained or
    ½ pound fresh mushrooms,
    sliced
2 cloves garlic,
    minced or mashed
1½ cups coarsely chopped onion
1 cup diagonally sliced celery
2 medium green peppers,
    cut in strips
2 (1-lb. 13-oz.) cans solid pack
    tomatoes
1 cup California Dry
    Red Table Wine
4 tablespoons cornstarch
    or 8 tablespoons flour
Water

Season meat with salt and pepper and brown in oil. Remove from pan.
Sauté mushrooms and garlic in drippings for 5 minutes; add onion and
celery and sauté until onion is clear. Stir in green pepper, tomatoes, wine
and browned meat. Cover and simmer until meat is tender, about 1½
hours. Mix cornstarch or flour with enough water to make a paste and stir
in. Bring to a boil and cook, stirring, about 5 minutes, until thickened.

My choice of wine to accompany this dish:
CALIFORNIA BURGUNDY *or* **VIN ROSÉ**

Veal with Peas

(4 SERVINGS)

Mrs. Robert Diana, Villa Armando, Pleasanton
This recipe must have originated among the frugal French peasantry, to whom veal and peas
are, after bread and onion soup, one of the most readily available and inexpensive food
combinations. Like most peasant dishes, it is both satisfying and filling.

3 pounds veal cutlets,
    one inch thick
3 tablespoons butter
    Salt, pepper
2 tablespoons flour
1 (10½-oz.) can beef broth
½ cup California Dry Sherry
    Pinch of thyme
2 tablespoons chopped parsley
1 (No. 303) can early peas

Cut veal into 1-inch cubes. Melt butter in saucepan, add veal, salt and
pepper, and brown meat well. Reduce heat, stir in flour. Remove from heat
and gradually stir in broth. Cook until sauce is medium-thick. Add wine,
thyme, parsley and peas. Continue cooking for about 15 minutes to blend
flavors.

My choice of wine to accompany this dish: **CALIFORNIA ROSÉ**

30

Braised Veal Roast

(6 TO 8 SERVINGS)

Mrs. Frank Lico, San Martin Vineyards, San Martin
Editor's note: This is a meal-on-a-platter, with the succulent veal surrounded by vegetables
and served with the sauce in which the meat was braised. Wine blends the many flavors
deliciously and seems to moderate the large amount of garlic.

4 to 6-pound boned veal
    shoulder or leg, rolled
Salt and pepper
¼ cup oil or butter
2 cups chopped onion
1 stalk celery, diced
1 cup diced carrots
6 peppercorns
1 bay leaf
¼ cup chopped parsley
3 cloves garlic, minced
½ cup California
    White Table Wine
1 (8-oz.) can tomato sauce
½ cup chicken broth
2 tablespoons oil or butter
2 large onions, cut in eighths
3 green peppers, cut in strips
2 sliced zucchini
1 small egg plant
    (sliced and cut in cubes)
1 (No. 303) can tomatoes
2 teaspoons salt

Season veal roast with salt and pepper. In deep, heavy skillet or Dutch oven, brown roast in oil or butter. Remove meat. In same pan, sauté chopped onion, celery and carrots for 5 minutes. Add peppercorns, bay leaf, parsley, 1 clove garlic, wine, tomato sauce and chicken broth. Cook over medium heat, uncovered, until liquid is reduced by half. Return roast to pan. Cover and bake in 350° oven 2 to 3 hours (about 30 minutes per pound). Add more broth or wine if necessary. About 20 minutes before roast is to be done, heat oil in skillet and sauté onions and green pepper until onion changes color. Add zucchini, egg plant and tomatoes. Season with salt. Cover and simmer 10 to 15 minutes. Add remaining garlic. Cook two minutes more. To serve, remove veal to a heated platter, surround with cooked vegetables. Sieve sauce in which meat was cooked and pour over meat or pass separately in a bowl.

 My choice of wine to accompany this dish:
A CALIFORNIA DRY WHITE TABLE WINE *or* ROSÉ

Roast Suckling Pig

(8 TO 10 SERVINGS)

Mrs. Alvin Ehrhardt, Allied Grape Growers, Fresno
I serve this with sauerkraut steamed in Champagne seasoned with garlic and coarse, black
pepper and with ice cold applesauce with a dash of cinnamon in it.

12 to 14 pound pig
5 tablespoons butter
2 medium onions, chopped
2 cloves garlic minced very fine
    Pig's liver, finely chopped
5 to 6 cups dry bread crumbs
¼ cup chopped parsley
1 tablespoon basil or rosemary
½ cup pistacho or pine nuts
½ cup California Sherry or
    Brandy
2 tablespoons butter

Melt the 5 tablespoons butter in a skillet and add onion and garlic. When they are soft, but not colored, add pig's liver and sauteé 1 to 2 minutes. Add cooked mixture to bread crumbs along with remaining ingredients; mix together well. Drain pig, pat dry, salt and pepper cavity lightly, stuff pig with mixture and sew it up securely. Rub skin well with oil. Sprinkle with salt, freshly ground pepper and a little oregano or sweet basil. Arrange pig on spit so that it is perfectly balanced. Roast 2 to 2½ hours, basting often with pan drippings. (Be sure to have a drip pan at least as long as the pig.) Roast it until it is crisp and beautifully browned. Serve with a sauce made with the pan drippings, ¼ lb. finely chopped parsley and 1 teaspoon dry mustard with seasoning to taste. Make a necklace of dark red Tokay grapes, two Tokay eyes and an apple in the mouth. To carve: cut along spinal column, cutting the pig in half. Remove each ham, slice the hams and cut through the ribs.

Editor's note: Such a festive dish almost requires that
CALIFORNIA CHAMPAGNE *be served with it.*

Stuffed Wild Ducks

(2 SERVINGS)

Mrs. Joseph Concannon, Jr., Concannon Vineyard, Livermore
This is the only way to cook duck. Since the birds are a meal in themselves I keep the menu simple with a tossed salad (with a light dressing) and a green vegetable. Dessert is usually sherbet or fruit.

DUCKS
2 wild ducks
  Orange juice
  Brandy

STUFFING
1 cup uncooked wild rice
4 cups boiling water
1 teaspoon salt
1 cup boiling chicken broth
4 tablespoons sweet butter
1½ tablespoons minced chives
1½ tablespoons minced parsley
1½ tablespoons minced small
    green onions
1½ tablespoons minced
    celery tops
1½ tablespoons minced
    sweet basil
1 teaspoon gin
  Salt and freshly ground
    pepper
  Pinch of nutmeg
  Duck giblets

BASTE AND SAUCE
1 cup orange juice
2 cups California
    Red Table Wine
2 teaspoons lemon juice
1 teaspoon grated orange rind
3 tablespoons curacao

Ducks: Rub drawn and cleaned ducks with an equal portion of orange juice and Brandy, inside and out. Set aside while preparing stuffing. **Stuffing:** Wash wild rice. In upper part of double boiler, over direct heat, add rice slowly to boiling, salted water. Cook 5 minutes. Add chicken broth, cover and continue cooking, over boiling water in lower part of double boiler, for 20 to 45 minutes until rice is tender. While rice is steaming, cream butter with chives, parsley, green onions, celery tops and basil. Season with gin, salt and ground pepper to taste, and a tiny pinch of nutmeg. Put the creamed butter mixture into large saucepan, melt and add wild rice and chopped giblets. Cook briefly, tossing rice until thoroughly mixed. Then stuff ducks with mixture. Put ducks into open roasting pan (I use a Dutch oven without top). **Baste and Sauce:** Pour into the pan with ducks, orange juice, 1 cup red wine, lemon juice and grated orange rind. Roast in 400° oven for 20 to 40 minutes until birds are tender, basting frequently. (It depends on age and size of birds.) Remove ducks to hot platter. Add remaining cup of red wine and curacao to juices in roaster, scraping pan well. Bring to boil on top of stove, stir briefly, then pour sauce over ducks and serve.

My choice of wine to accompany this dish:
CALIFORNIA CABERNET SAUVIGNON *or* **PETITE SIRAH**

Chicken Tortilla

(8 SERVINGS)

Mrs. Reginald Gianelli, East-Side Winery, Lodi
Editor's note: This casserole dish is assembled in layers—chicken, tortillas, cheese and green chiles—with a dry white table wine as the seasoning that blends the unusual flavors together. It's ideal for the main dish of a buffet supper

4 whole chicken breasts
   (or 8 halves)
1 (10½-oz.) can
   cream of celery soup
1 (10½-oz.) can
   cream of mushroom soup
1¼ cups California Chablis or
   other White Table Wine
1 large onion, diced
12 tortillas
1 (7-oz.) can green chiles
   (seeds removed)
1 pound Cheddar cheese,
   shredded

Wrap chicken breasts in foil and bake 1 hour in a moderately hot oven (400°). Cool, bone and break into large pieces. Mix soups with wine and onion. Cut tortillas and chiles in strips. Layer ingredients in a casserole, starting with small amount of liquid and ending with cheese, in this order: liquid, tortillas, chicken, chile, cheese. Bake uncovered in a moderate oven (350°) for 1 hour.

Editor's note: Serve a CALIFORNIA CHABLIS, ROSÉ, or a light red wine such as GRIGNOLINO with this dish.

Epicurean Chicken Livers

(4 SERVINGS)

Mrs. James Gott, United Vintners, San Francisco
We tried unsuccessfully for many years to obtain a chicken liver recipe from a fine restaurant at Lake Tahoe. Finally we gave up and developed this recipe.
We, and our guests, think it is wonderful. With the livers we serve a rice casserole, Chinese pea pods, and limestone lettuce salad.

1½ pounds frying chicken livers
   Flour
5 tablespoons butter
   Garlic powder, salt and
   pepper
½ pound fresh mushrooms,
   sauteed in butter
⅓ cup California Dry Sherry
⅓ cup chopped green onion
⅓ cup chopped fresh parsley

Soak livers in cold water for 30 minutes. Drain and dry on paper towels. Very lightly dust livers with flour. Melt butter in frying pan which can be covered tightly. Brown livers quickly over fairly high heat so livers remain pink inside. Reduce heat to low. Add seasonings, sautéed mushrooms and Sherry. Stir until slightly thickened (more Sherry may be added as required). Sprinkle onions and parsley over top. Cover and steam for two minutes. Serve immediately.

My choice of wine to accompany this dish: **CALIFORNIA CHABLIS**

Chicken Hearts in Sour Cream

(3 TO 4 SERVINGS)

Mrs. Philip Smyser, Wine Advisory Board, San Francisco
I serve this over noodles with a salad and homemade muffins.

1 pound chicken hearts,
    split lengthwise
½ pound fresh mushrooms,
    halved
½ green pepper, chopped
1 pimiento, chopped
½ onion, chopped
3 tablespoons butter
    Garlic salt, salt, pepper,
    basil, spiced pepper,
    oregano, poultry seasoning
    to taste
¼ cup California
    White Table Wine
2 cups medium white sauce
    (homemade, canned or use
    a sauce mix)
½ cup dairy sour cream

Sauté chicken hearts, onion, green pepper, mushrooms, and pimiento in butter until almost done. Add wine and seasonings. Cook until tender. Mix white sauce and sour cream with the above. Serve.

My choice of wine to accompany this dish:
CALIFORNIA WHITE TABLE WINE

Franzia Baked Chicken

(4 TO 6 SERVINGS)

Mrs. Frank Franzia, Jr., Franzia Brothers Winery, Ripon
I threw this recipe together one night when I was in a rush to get dinner started. It turned out so well, and was so simple to make, I now serve it often—even when I have plenty of time.

1 (3-lb.) broiling chicken
    Salt, pepper, garlic powder
1 (4-oz.) can mushroom pieces
1 medium onion, cut in wedges
¼ cup melted butter
5 medium potatoes, sliced in
    ¼-inch slices
½ cup California Sauterne
½ cup water

Rub whole chicken with seasonings all over and in cavity. Tuck mushrooms between thighs and breast, put remainder in cavity along with onion. Brush entire chicken with melted butter then pour rest into chicken cavity. Bake in moderate oven (350°) for 30 minutes, then place sliced potatoes around chicken in pan. Mix wine and water together and pour over all. Bake for 30 minutes more, basting once.

My choice of wine to accompany this dish: **CALIFORNIA CHABLIS**

Chicken with Burgundy and Black Cherry Sauce

(4 SERVINGS)

Mrs. Philip Smyser, Wine Advisory Board, San Francisco
This is an impressive party dish, although it is quite easy to prepare. With it we serve rice
pilaf, a steamed green vegetable like broccoli with lemon and mayonnaise sauce,
and something elegant for dessert.

1 (2½ to 3½-lb.) frying chicken,
   cut up
1 (20-oz.) can dark, sweet,
   pitted cherries
   (reserve juice)
1 cup California Burgundy
3 tablespoons lemon juice
2 or 3 cloves garlic, crushed
¼ teaspoon ground ginger
½ teaspoon oregano
2 teaspoons salt
   Dash pepper
1 chicken bouillon cube
¼ cup shortening or oil
⅓ cup cornstarch
   Parsley

Wash and dry chicken. Drain cherries and save liquid. Into large kettle combine cherry juice, wine, lemon juice, garlic, ginger, oregano, salt, pepper and bouillon cube. Add chicken and simmer until tender (about one hour). Remove chicken, drain, brown in oil. Mix cornstarch with cold water to make a paste. Add to sauce, cook and stir until thickened. Add chicken and cherries to sauce, simmer till cherries are hot through. To serve, heap chicken on platter, top with cherries and sauce. Garnish with lots of parsley. Serve extra sauce on the side.

My choice of wine to accompany this dish:
CALIFORNIA BURGUNDY *or* **SPARKLING BURGUNDY**

Honolulu Chicken

(6 TO 8 SERVINGS)

Mr. and Mrs. Rudy Windmiller, Almaden Vineyards, San Francisco
This is our own combination, especially appreciated because it does not have any added fat.
Editor's note: A touch of spice, and the use of red table wine for flavoring is unusual and good.

2 large fryers, cut up
2 cups California Burgundy
   or Claret
½ cup soy sauce
1 teaspoon ground ginger
½ teaspoon nutmeg
1 tablespoon sugar
1 teaspoon grated orange rind,
   fresh or dried
1 (8½-oz.) can pineapple slices
   Crushed garlic or garlic salt
   to taste

Place chicken, skin side down, in oven pan (about 16 x 11 x 2½ inches). Prepare marinade of wine and all other ingredients including syrup from pineapple slices. (Keep slices for garnishing.) Pour marinade over chickens. Leave several hours or overnight in refrigerator. Bake 1½ to 2 hours or just until tender in moderate oven (350°), turning pieces after one hour. About 15 minutes before serving, put quartered pineapple slices into the baking dish; use later for garnishing; add sprig of parsley on plate. This is also excellent for serving cold because the marinade jells.

My choice of wine to accompany this dish:
CALIFORNIA JOHANNISBERG RIESLING *or* **GEWURZTRAMINER**

Delicious Chicken Casserole

(5 SERVINGS)

Mrs. Aldo Nerelli, Pesenti Winery, Templeton
Editor's note: This chicken casserole is easy to prepare and to serve because it's made of chicken breasts—one for each serving. The seasonings are subtle so they don't overpower the dry white wine that makes this dish outstanding.

5 large chicken breasts, boned
1 teaspoon monosodium
  glutamate
1 teaspoon salt
  Pepper
  Flour
⅓ cup butter
1 cup fresh mushrooms
¼ cup chopped green onions,
  including tops
1 clove garlic, thinly sliced
½ cup California
  White Table Wine
1 (7-oz.) can artichoke hearts

Sprinkle chicken with monosodium glutamte, salt and pepper and coat well with flour. Brown in ¼ cup of the butter. Remove chicken, add remaining butter; brown mushrooms, onions and garlic. Return chicken to pan and add wine and simmer gently 45 minutes or until tender. Add drained artichoke hearts and heat thoroughly.

My choice of wine to accompany this dish:
CALIFORNIA DRY SAUTERNE *or* **CHABLIS**

Chicken Stroganoff

(6 SERVINGS)

Kelli Ellis, Almaden Vineyards, San Francisco
Editor's note: Wine, sour cream and mushrooms give this chicken specialty excellent flavor. As an alternate method of cooking, add wine and mushrooms together, simmer 25 minutes, then add sour cream and simmer 10 minutes more. There's less chance for the cream to curdle in this shorter cooking time.

8 chicken breasts, boned
2 eggs, beaten
  Salt and pepper
4 tablespoons oil
⅓ cup California
  White Table Wine
1 pint dairy sour cream
1 cup fresh sliced mushrooms
  Water

Have butcher bone chicken breasts. Roll the chicken in beaten eggs, and seasonings. Brown in oil (or use half oil and half butter) slowly on all sides, approximately 15 minutes per side at 250°. Turn heat down to "simmer" and let the meat set for 10 minutes. Pour wine over, and allow to stand for a few minutes. Then stir in sour cream and mushrooms. Add water as desired so the sauce is consistency of gravy. Allow meat and sauce to simmer for 45 minutes, and serve over noodles.

Editor's note: Try a **CALIFORNIA GEWURZTRAMINER** *or* **PINOT CHARDONNAY** *with this dish. Either one goes very well with it.*

Chicken à la Waleski

(4 SERVINGS)

Mrs. Geneva Shuflin, Wine Institute, San Francisco
This is a successful copy of a heavenly dish served at L'Omelette in Los Altos, California.
With it I serve rice steamed in chicken broth, tossed green salad with a mild dressing,
French bread to soak up some of the delicious gravy and flaming Mandarin oranges over
vanilla ice cream for dessert.

CHICKEN
2 broiler-fryer chickens, cut up
2 carrots
2 onions
2 (13¾-oz.) cans chicken broth
4 tablespoons chopped parsley
2 pinches thyme
  Bay leaf
2 whole cloves
4 peppercorns
4 tablespoons butter

SAUCE
6 tablespoons butter
4 tablespoons flour
1 cup California
    White Table Wine
2 egg yolks
4 tablespoons heavy cream
1 pound fresh mushrooms
4 tablespoons butter
  Juice of 2 lemons

Chicken: Simmer chicken pieces gently until tender with carrots, onions, chicken broth, parsley, thyme, bay leaf, cloves and peppercorns. When chicken is done, drain and save broth. Dry chicken on a cloth and brown in the 4 tablespoons butter. **Sauce:** Blend 6 tablespoons butter with flour and stir over heat for a few minutes. Gradually add 2 cups reserved chicken broth and wine, stirring into a smooth sauce; bring to a boil. Remove the fat and strain through a sieve. Let sauce simmer and reduce. Add egg yolks mixed with cream. Sauté mushrooms in butter until a light brown. Place browned chicken in serving dish, place mushrooms all around, cover with a little gravy. Pour the lemon juice over all. Serve remaining gravy separately.

 My choice of wine to accompany this dish:
CALIFORNIA EMERALD RIESLING *or* CHENIN BLANC

Blazing Chicken

(4 SERVINGS)

Mrs. Alfred Fromm, Fromm & Sichel, San Francisco
Editor's note: Like many fine old recipes, this one uses a wine glass measurement.
It adds a certain flair to the cooking and flaming. In standardized measurement, a wine glass
measurement equals about one-third cup.

¾ cup sweet butter
1 roasting chicken (about 3 lbs.)
1 wineglass California Brandy
1 wineglass California Port
1 tablespoon flour
1½ cups heavy cream, warmed
  Salt and pepper

Butter a baking dish and put remainder of butter inside chicken. Bake in 350° oven, turning the bird first on one side and then on the other. Baste frequently. At the end of 35 minutes, pour Brandy over chicken. Light it and when the blaze is burning brightly extinguish it with the glass of Port. Finish baking the chicken, approximately 30 minutes longer. Remove chicken and keep warm. Place baking dish over medium heat on top of stove, stir in flour, cook for a minute or so, then add the cream. Stir just a moment and pour over the chicken, when served.

 Editor's note: **CALIFORNIA PINOT CHARDONNAY**
is a distinguished partner for this dish.

Chicken Breasts Mandarin

(6 SERVINGS)

Mrs. Frank Bartholomew, Buena Vista Winery, Sonoma
Mrs. Frederick Voigt, who is a frequent visitor at Buena Vista Vineyards has been kind enough to share one of her favorite recipes with us.

3 chicken breasts, halved
Flour
½ teaspoon monosodium glutamate
Pepper
3 tablespoons butter
¾ cup chicken broth
½ cup California White Table Wine
3 tablespoons cornstarch
2 teaspoons soy sauce
½ teaspoon grated orange rind
¾ teaspoon paprika
1 (11-oz.) can Mandarin orange segments and juice

Skin chicken; dust with flour seasoned with monosodium glutamate and pepper. Brown in melted butter; place in baking dish. Add chicken broth to pan drippings; simmer while scraping up crusty bits from bottom and sides. Pour wine in small covered jar with cornstarch; shake smooth. Add to sauce; stir until smooth. Add remaining ingredients, except oranges, and simmer until well blended and slightly thickened. Pour sauce over chicken. Cover. Bake at 325° for 45 minutes or until tender. Add drained orange segments last 10 minutes.

My choice of wine to accompany this dish:
CALIFORNIA PINOT CHARDONNAY

Squabs in White Wine

(6 TO 8 SERVINGS)

Mrs. August Sebastiani, Samuele Sebastiani Winery, Sonoma
Editor's note: Either squabs or small chickens, cooked whole are good seasoned in this way with white wine and shallots. Mrs. Sebastiani says that an extra special touch for this dish is wild rice. Also a watercress salad in season is an excellent addition to this meal.

6 squabs or small chickens
3 tablespoons olive oil
3 tablespoons butter
2 cups California White Table Wine
6 squab livers
2 chicken livers
8 shallots, finely chopped
1 (8-oz.) can sliced button mushrooms
Salt and pepper
Chopped parsley

Truss squabs. In a large heavy skillet, heat olive oil and butter and brown birds lightly on both sides. Add wine and salt and pepper to taste. Cover the pan loosely and cook birds for 15 minutes. Add birds' livers, chicken livers, shallots and mushrooms with their liquid, and cook this mixture, covered, for 15 minutes longer, or until the birds are tender. Transfer the birds to a heated platter, pour the pan juices over them, and sprinkle with chopped parsley.

My choice of wine to accompany this dish:
CALIFORNIA GREEN HUNGARIAN

Petite Poulette au Vin

(4 SERVINGS)

Mrs. Richard Peterson, Beaulieu Vineyard, Rutherford
Editor's note: One teaspoon of mixed dry Italian herbs substitutes for the Fines Herbs in this recipe, though fresh herbs from the garden are, of course, delightful whenever available.

2 chickens, cut in halves
½ cup oil
½ cup butter
1 cup California Dry Sherry
　Fines Herbs
　Paprika
　Salt and pepper
　Sautéed mushrooms

Put oil in large baking dish, arrange chicken, dot with butter and pour on Sherry. Add seasonings. Bake in moderate oven (350°) 45 minutes to 1 hour. Garnish with mushrooms.

Editor's note: **CALIFORNIA JOHANNISBERG RIESLING** *is a wonderful accompaniment to this chicken dish.*

Pheasant Surprise

(4 TO 5 SERVINGS)

Mrs. Rene Baillif, Concannon Vineyard, San Francisco
Pheasant cooked in this way makes a sumptuous dish. Start the meal with sliced tomatoes and anchovies. Serve wild rice with the pheasant and Camembert and pears for dessert.

¼ cup oil
¼ cup butter
2 pheasants boned, skinned
　　and cut in pieces
　Flour
2 shallots, minced
½ pound mushrooms, sliced
1 cup bouillon or chicken broth
1 cup California Dry Sherry
2 jiggers (¼ cup) California
　　Brandy
1 small stalk celery
1 sprig parsley
1 small green onion

Heat the oil and butter in a deep skillet or Dutch oven over medium heat. Slightly coat pheasant pieces with a little flour, brown them evenly to a golden color, add shallots, mushrooms, bouillon, Sherry, Brandy, celery, parsley and onion. Cover and cook slowly 1½ to 2 hours.

My choice of wine to accompany this dish: **CALIFORNIA PETITE SIRAH**

Mandarin Pheasant

(6 SERVINGS)

Mrs. Jack Farrior, Jr., Almaden Vineyards, Los Gatos
We like this pheasant with wild rice, Green Peppers Florentine, (page 64)
a tossed green salad, and fried apples.

- 6 pheasant breasts, split
- 2 (10½-oz.) cans chicken broth
- ⅓ cup soy sauce
- 1 clove garlic
- 1 teaspoon fresh grated ginger
- 1 (6-oz.) can frozen concentrated orange juice
- 1 cup brown sugar
- 1 teaspoon salt
- 1 cup California Chablis
- 2 (11-oz.) cans Mandarin oranges, drained

Place breasts in large baking dish with all ingredients except oranges and cover. Bake in moderate oven (350°) for 1½ hours. Arrange orange segments over pheasant breasts. Continue baking uncovered for ½ hour or until there is a golden glaze.

 My choice of wine to accompany this dish: **CALIFORNIA CHABLIS**

Blossom Hill Pheasant

(2 GENEROUS SERVINGS)

Mrs. E. Jeff Barnette, Martini & Prati Winery, Santa Rosa
We serve this pheasant with asparagus or another green vegetable, and Lemon Meringue Pie.

- 1 pheasant
- 2 cups California Red Table Wine
- 5 tablespoons melted butter or margarine
- Salt and pepper
- 3 stalks celery, sliced
- 3 sprigs parsley, chopped
- ½ cup each, sliced onions and carrots
- 2 slices bacon
- 1 cup light cream
- 2 tablespoons currant jelly

Wash and drain pheasant. Marinate several hours or overnight in wine, turning several times. Remove and dry with paper towels. Brush inside and out with melted butter. Season with salt and pepper. In 450° oven, roast pheasant, 20 minutes, until golden brown. Place celery, parsley, onions, carrots and bacon in bottom of casserole. Place pheasant on top, add about half of the wine marinade and bake covered in 350° oven for 30 minutes. Pour cream over the bird and bake covered until tender. Remove cover from pan and return to very hot oven (500°) until brown, about 10 minutes. Baste several times. Strain the pan gravy and mix with currant jelly, beating until smooth. Serve the gravy separately.

My choice of wine to accompany this dish: **CALIFORNIA CABERNET SAUVIGNON, PINOT NOIR** *or* **SPARKLING BURGUNDY**

41

Roast Stuffed Pheasant

(8 SERVINGS)

Mr. Robert Diana, Villa Armando, Pleasanton
Editor's note: The sausage and other seasonings give these whole roasted pheasants a
definite Italian character. The birds are moist and very flavorful.

STUFFING
¾ pound Italian sweet sausage
½ cup uncooked wild rice
2 slices bread
¼ cup milk
¼ cup olive oil
7 tablespoons butter, melted
1 ounce salt pork, diced
¼ pound onions, diced
1 bay leaf, crumbled
1 small garlic clove, mashed
½ cup California
        White Table Wine
2 eggs, lightly beaten
½ cup chopped parsley
¼ cup grated Parmesan cheese

PHEASANTS
2 pheasants
3 thin slices salt pork
¼ teaspoon minced fresh
        rosemary
Salt and pepper
¼ cup hot chicken broth

Prepare Stuffing: Remove casing from sausage and cut meat into 1-inch pieces. Soak rice in lukewarm water for 15 minutes, then drain and cook in lightly salted water for about 20 minutes or until tender, but not mushy; drain. Soak the bread in milk, squeeze out the liquid and crumble the bread. Combine 3 tablespoons of the oil and 4 tablespoons of the butter and the diced salt pork in a skillet; heat. Add the onions and sauté to medium brown. Add sausage pieces, chopped giblets, the bay leaf and garlic. Cook 20 minutes. Add the wine, cover and cook 3 minutes. Remove mixture from the heat and cool 10 minutes. Take the ingredients from the skillet; chop very fine. Do not lose juices. Place all back in the skillet, add the bread, beaten eggs, parsley, cheese and drained rice. Mix well.
Pheasants: Fill the birds with the stuffing. Truss the birds and place them breast side down in oiled roasting pan. Roast at 450° for 10 minutes. Turn the birds and cover breasts with the sliced salt pork. Sprinkle seasonings over the birds and pat remaining oil on parts not covered with salt pork. Reduce heat to slow (300°) and cook 45 minutes basting occasionally. The whole cooking time should not be longer than 1 hour. Remove from oven and keep warm. Discard fat from roasting pan. Add remaining butter and hot broth to the drippings in the pan and simmer for 10 minutes until mixture is reduced to a gravy. Strain, spoon gravy over birds and serve immediately.

My choice of wine to accompany this dish:
CALIFORNIA BURGUNDY *or* **BARBERA**

Theresa's Sherry-Flavored Chicken

(3 SERVINGS)

Mrs. Enzo Casazza, Cambiaso Winery and Vineyards, Healdsburg
This is my mother's recipe. We serve it over steamed rice with a sprinkle of cheese.
It's even delicious reheated the next day. Editor's note: The Sherry flavor is subtle. If you
like it more dominant, increase the Sherry ingredient to ⅓ cup and cut the water to ⅔ cup.

1 (2½-lb.) chicken, cut up
½ cup butter
1 medium onion, sliced
⅓ cup California Sherry or
        Marsala
1 cup water
1 (8-oz.) can tomato sauce
½ teaspoon paprika
Salt and pepper

Fry chicken slowly in butter till browned on all sides. Remove chicken to oven baking dish, sauté onion in butter in which chicken has been browned and add wine, water, tomato sauce and paprika. Bring to a boil, add seasonings and pour over chicken. Bake 50 to 60 minutes at 375°.

My choice of wine to accompany this dish:
CALIFORNIA CHABLIS *or* **GRENACHE ROSÉ**

Flaming Cornish Hens

(6 SERVINGS)

Mrs. Earl G. Harrah, Wine Advisory Board, San Francisco
Flaming Cornish Hens is the main dish of our favorite Epicurean dinner. I enjoy cooking and serving this menu on very special occasions and Earl enjoys serving it at the table. First there is a crab and avocado cocktail seasoned lightly with Sherry, then come the birds, garnished with spiced peaches. The vegetable is green beans amandine.
Strawberries in Champagne top off the meal.

6 **Rock Cornish Hens**
    (14 to 16 oz. each),
    fresh or frozen
1 **tablespoon salt**
2 **(6-oz.) packages wild rice**
    (6 cups cooked)
3 **(2½-oz.) cans whole button**
    mushrooms, drained
1 **cup finely chopped onion**
1 **cup finely chopped celery**
½ **cup butter or margarine**
1 **cup California**
    White Table Wine
    Salt and freshly ground
    pepper
    Melted butter
    California Brandy
    Spiced peaches
    Wine gravy (below)

WINE GRAVY
2 **tablespoons butter or**
    margarine
½ **cup flour**
¾ **cup California**
    White Table Wine
¾ **cup water**
1 **(4-oz.) can mushrooms**
2 **tablespoons chopped parsley**
1 **tablespoon chopped onion**
½ **tablespoon paprika**
½ **teaspoon salt**
¼ **teaspoon freshly ground**
    pepper
1 **cup dairy sour cream**

Wash birds and dry thoroughly, inside and out. Rub inside cavity of each with ½ teaspoon salt. Prepare wild rice stuffing: Cook rice according to package directions. Sauté drained mushrooms, onion, and celery in melted butter. Then add to cooked rice along with the wine and seasonings. Mix lightly with a fork. Stuff body and neck cavity of each bird loosely with stuffing. (A scant cup stuffing for each is usually sufficient.) Skewer openings together. Brush outside of hens with melted butter. Place on rack in shallow pan and bake in moderate oven (350°) until tender, about 1¼ hours. Brush with additional butter as needed. **Wine Gravy:** Melt Butter or margarine in pan in which birds were cooked. Blend in flour. Mix wine and water and gradually add to flour-butter mixture, stirring constantly. Cook until thick and smooth. Add mushrooms with liquid, parsley, onion, paprika, salt and pepper. Just before serving add sour cream at room temperature. Heat thoroughly, but do not boil. Makes about 3½ cups wine gravy. To serve: Place birds in a circle on a large fire-proof serving plate (a round chop plate is best). Garnish with spiced peaches. Pour warmed Brandy over hens and peaches, ignite and bring to the table in flames.* Serve with wine gravy.

My choice of wine to accompany this dish: **CALIFORNIA SPARKLING BURGUNDY, CHAMPAGNE** *or* **CABERNET SAUVIGNON**
Editor's note: White and wild-rice mix may be substituted for the wild rice specified in this recipe, or brown rice mixed with a small amount of wild rice may also be used.
* Note: Be sure to warm the Brandy in a double boiler over hot water, never in an open pot over flame.

Fish and Shellfish

Sole with Shrimp and Crab Filling

(6 SERVINGS)

Mrs. Morris Katz, Paul Masson Vineyards, Saratoga
Editor's note: Sole fillets form rolls around a savory shrimp and crab stuffing.
The wine sauce tops each serving.

FISH
3 large fillets of sole
   (1½ lbs.)
½ teaspoon salt
⅛ teaspoon white pepper
  Filling (below)
  Wine Sauce (below)
  Melted butter
  Parsley for garnish
12 whole shrimp for garnish
FILLING
1½ teaspoons butter
1½ tablespoons flour
½ cup milk
½ cup flaked crabmeat,
   canned or fresh
½ cup cooked chopped shrimp,
   canned or fresh
¼ cup chopped celery
¼ cup chopped green onions
1 teaspoon chopped parsley
½ teaspoon salt
  SAUCE
1 tablespoon butter
1 teaspoon flour
½ cup California
   White Table Wine
½ cup light cream
¼ teaspoon salt
  Dash pepper
  Hot sauce to taste
2 egg yolks, lightly beaten
1 teaspoon lemon juice

Fish: Season the fillets with salt and pepper. Lay flat on baking sheet.
Filling: Melt butter and stir in flour. Gradually add milk and cook, stirring constantly, until sauce thickens. Remove from heat and stir in crabmeat, shrimp, celery, onions, parsley and salt. Divide the filling equally among the fillets, spreading it generously. Roll the fillets carefully and secure with picks. Cut each roll in half and place in shallow baking dish. Bake in moderately hot oven (400°) for 30 minutes. Baste often with melted butter. Meanwhile, prepare **Wine Sauce:** In upper part of double boiler, melt butter, stir in flour, then gradually mix in wine and cream. Season with salt and pepper. Heat over boiling water, stirring constantly, about 5 minutes, until sauce thickens slightly. Add a few spoonfuls of hot sauce to the slightly beaten egg yolks. Then stir egg mixture into sauce. Continue cooking a few minutes longer, stirring, until eggs thicken sauce. Add lemon juice and pour over sole rolls on serving plates. Garnish with parsley and whole cooked shrimp.

My choice of wine to accompany this dish:
CALIFORNIA EMERALD RIESLING

Oysters Provençales

(AS FIRST COURSE: 4 SERVINGS. AS MAIN DISH: 2 SERVINGS)

Mrs. Leon S. Peters, Valley Foundry, Fresno

1 onion, chopped
3 tablespoons margarine or
    butter
4 tablespoons flour
2 cups rich milk
¾ teaspoon salt
¼ teaspoon paprika
    Dash pepper
½ teaspoon monosodium
    glutamate
    Garlic salt to taste
3 tablespoons finely chopped
    parsley
¼ cup California
    White Table Wine
2 (8-oz.) cans oysters

Sauté onions in margarine. Toss with flour and gradually add milk and keep stirring. Add seasonings, parsley and wine. The sauce can be covered and set aside until one-half hour before you are ready to serve. When ready to serve, drain oysters, reserving liquid, and place them in individual casseroles. Reheat cream sauce with broth from oysters, and pour over oysters. Bake in 300° oven about 20 minutes.

My choice of wine to accompany this dish:
CALIFORNIA GREY RIESLING *or* **EMERALD RIESLING**

Salmon Mousse

(6 SERVINGS)

Mrs. Don Rudolph, Cresta Blanca Wine Company, Livermore
Editor's note: This elegant salmon mousse is made in two parts then layered in a ring mold.

PART I
1 (1-lb.) can salmon
½ cup lemon juice
1 envelope unflavored gelatin
2 tablespoons water
½ cup California
    White Table Wine
PART II
2 egg yolks
1½ tablespoons soft butter
    or margarine
½ teaspoon flour
1 teaspoon salt
2 teaspoons sugar
1 teaspoon Worcestershire
    sauce
1 teaspoon dry mustard
1 teaspoon grated onion
⅛ teaspoon cayenne
½ teaspoon fresh dill,
    dried dill-weed or
    finely chopped parsley
¾ cup milk
1 envelope unflavored gelatin
¼ cup California
    White Table Wine

Part I: If you have a blender, put the whole can of salmon, bones and all, in blender jar. Add lemon juice. Blend until smooth. If you have no blender, remove bones and any skin, and with a fork, flake the salmon into tiny pieces. Soften gelatin in water for five minutes. Dissolve gelatin over hot water. Allow to cool, then combine with wine and salmon. Chill while preparing second part. **Part II:** In upper part of one-quart double boiler over hot water, beat egg yolks. Smooth together the butter and flour and add to egg yolks, stirring constantly. Add salt, sugar, Worcestershire sauce, mustard, onion, cayenne, dill and milk. Add gelatin that has been soaked for a few minutes in wine. Stir until gelatin is dissolved. Let mixture cool until slightly set. Rub a 1½-quart ring mold with cooking oil. Pour in one-third of cooked gelatin mixture. Let stand 5 minutes. Add ½ of salmon mixture. Repeat with gelatin and fish until all are used. Pour last of gelatin on top. Chill until firm, about 3 hours. To serve, unmold on a chilled platter. If desired, garnish with watercress or surround with cocktail crackers.

Editor's note: Either **CALIFORNIA PINOT CHARDONNAY** *or* **CHABLIS** *would be excellent wine accompaniments for this dish.*

Fillet of Sole Florentine
(4 SERVINGS)

Mrs. Leon S. Peters, Valley Foundry, Fresno

4 tablespoons flour
4 tablespoons butter
    or margarine
2 cups rich milk
¾ teaspoon salt
    Pepper
½ teaspoon curry powder
    or more to taste
1 (10-oz.) package frozen
    chopped spinach
2 pounds fillet of sole
½ cup California
    White Table Wine
¼ cup water
    Salt
    Parmesan cheese

Make standard cream sauce by blending flour with butter or margarine, then add milk and stir constantly until thick and smooth. Season with salt, pepper and curry powder to taste. Set aside. This can be made ahead of time and reheated when ready to use. Cook spinach in very little water; drain, pressing out excess water. Simmer the sole in wine and water, in a covered fryer about 5 minutes. Butter individual casseroles or one shallow casserole. Place spinach on bottom, salt lightly, lift fish carefully and place on top of spinach. Add some sauce that fish has been cooked in to the cream sauce and reheat. Sauce should be medium thick. Correct seasoning if necessary and pour over fish. Sprinkle Parmesan cheese over top and bake in 300° oven about 20 minutes until bubbly. Put under broiler to brown lightly.

 My choice of wine to accompany this dish:
CALIFORNIA GEWURZTRAMINER

Stuffed Fish Rolls
(6 SERVINGS)

Mrs. Herbert L. Grosswendt, Brookside Vineyard Company, Agoura

½ tablespoon minced onion
2 tablespoons butter
6 thin white fish fillets
    (about 1½ pounds)
⅛ pound fresh mushrooms,
    sliced thin (about ¼ cup)
⅛ pound tiny cooked shrimp
    (about ⅔ cup)
    Salt and cracked pepper
½ pint dairy sour cream
¼ cup California Chablis
    Paprika

Cook onion in butter until transparent. Sprinkle fish fillets with mushrooms, shrimp, onion, salt and pepper. Roll up fillets and secure with picks. Put in greased baking dish and top with sour cream thinned with wine. Sprinkle with paprika, and bake in moderate oven (350°) for 20 minutes or until fish flakes easily.

 My choice of wine to accompany this dish: **CALIFORNIA CHABLIS**

Winemasters' Swordfish
(6 SERVINGS)

Mrs. Robert M. Ivie, Guild Wine Company, San Francisco

6 swordfish steaks
    (about 1 inch thick)
1 tablespoon minced onion
1 teaspoon oregano
2 tablespoons chopped parsley
½ teaspoon salt
    Freshly ground pepper
    to taste
2 tablespoons lemon juice
1 cup California Sauterne

Marinate swordfish steaks for two hours or longer in a mixture of all remaining ingredients, turning occasionally. For barbecuing: When coals are ready place steaks on buttered rack. Cook about 5 minutes on each side, using the marinade to brush on heavily during cooking. For broiling: Place steaks on buttered rack 3 inches from heat. Do the same as for barbecuing. Swordfish should be golden brown and firm, but flaky, when done.

Editor's note: Any **DRY CALIFORNIA WHITE TABLE WINE**
is a good choice to accompany this dish.

Artichoke and Shrimp Casserole

(4 SERVINGS)

Mrs. Jack Welsch, The Christian Brothers, San Francisco
This is a slight variation of a dish reported to have been a favorite of Adlai Stevenson, former U.S. Ambassador to the United Nations. It is also one of our favorites, and I have made it for just family and for large parties. I serve it buffet style at parties in a Dansk casserole, with a matching one for Turmeric rice.

1 (8-oz.) package frozen artichoke hearts, cooked according to directions
1 pound medium-size fresh shrimp, cooked and cleaned
¼ pound fresh or canned mushrooms
1 (5-oz.) can water chestnuts
2 tablespoons butter
1 tablespoon Worcestershire sauce
¼ cup California Dry Sherry
1½ cups medium cream sauce (made with 3 tablespoons flour and light cream)
¼ cup grated Parmesan cheese
Salt and pepper
Dash of paprika

Cook and drain artichoke hearts and arrange in buttered casserole. Spread the cooked shrimp over them. Sauté sliced mushrooms for 6 minutes and add them to baking dish. Slice water chestnuts and add to baking dish. Add Worcestershire sauce, salt, pepper and Sherry to cream sauce and pour over contents of baking dish. Sprinkle the top with Parmesan cheese, dust with paprika, and bake for 20 to 25 minutes in 375° oven.

 My choice of wine to accompany this dish: **CALIFORNIA CHENIN BLANC**

Crab Coquille

(4 TO 6 SERVINGS)

Mrs. Arthur Caputi, Jr., E. & J. Gallo Winery, Modesto
We serve this crab dish with rice pilaf, homemade yeast rolls and green salad with Parmesan cheese dressing. Because this is a fairly simple meal, we prefer to serve a rich dessert, such as a chocolate soufflé with creme chantilly or chocolate sauce.

⅔ cup California Sauterne, Chablis, or other white table wine
⅓ cup water
1 sprig parsley
1 small onion, halved
2 (7½-oz.) cans Alaskan King Crab
2 tablespoons butter
¼ pound mushrooms, sliced
2 tablespoons flour
1 (10-oz.) can condensed cream of chicken soup
⅓ cup heavy cream
2 tablespoons lemon juice
4 to 6 baked pastry shells

Combine wine, water, parsley and onion and heat to boiling. Add crab and simmer 5 minutes. Drain, reserving 1 cup of the liquid. Cut the crab meat into bite-size pieces. Melt butter in saucepan, add mushrooms and brown lightly. Blend in flour. Gradually add soup, cream and lemon juice; cook, stirring constantly, until thickened. Gradually stir in the reserved wine broth. Fold in crab. Spoon into pastry shells.

 My choice of wine to accompany this dish: **CALIFORNIA RIESLING**

Wine Baked Fish

(6 SERVINGS)

Mrs. Frank Franzia, Sr., Franzia Brothers Winery, Ripon

2½ pounds fillets of halibut
    or other white fish
½ cup halved mushroom caps
1 carrot, diced
2 tablespoons chopped leek
    or onion
¼ cup olive oil
1 cup California
    White Table Wine
½ cup water or fish stock
    Salt and pepper

Place fillets in well-greased pan. Sauté mushrooms, carrot and leek in olive oil for 5 minutes. Add wine, water. Season to taste. Simmer until the vegetables are tender, but still firm. Remove vegetables, reserving liquid, and arrange on top of fish; cover. Bake in moderate oven (350°) 15 to 20 minutes. Boil the liquid briskly to reduce by half; pour over fish just before serving.

My choice of wine to accompany this dish:
CALIFORNIA CHABLIS *or* **SAUTERNE**

Scampi Delectable

(3 TO 4 SERVINGS)

Mrs. Maury Baldwin, Owens-Illinois Glass Co., Sacramento

2 pounds fresh jumbo prawns
3 cloves garlic, finely minced
¼ teaspoon salt
2 tablespoons chopped parsley
¼ cup olive oil
¼ cup melted butter
½ cup California White Wine
2 tablespoons lemon juice
⅛ teaspoon freshly ground
    pepper

Shell and devein prawns, leave tail on. Split lengthwise, 1 inch from head, forming butterfly. Combine remaining ingredients and mix well. Marinate prawns in mixture for several hours. Arrange prawns in single layer in shallow pan. Pour remaining sauce over. Broil for 6 to 8 minutes, 3 inches from heat. Remove prawns to warm platter and pour drippings from pan over all. Be sure to remove from broiler while prawns are still "chewy"; do not overcook.

My choice of wine to accompany this dish:
CALIFORNIA GREY RIESLING *or* **GREEN HUNGARIAN**

Baked Striped Bass Fillets

(4 TO 6 SERVINGS)

Miss Marjorie Lumm, Wine Institute, San Francisco

Leon Adams, author of "Striped Bass Fishing" and "The Commonsense Book of Wine," generously shares his catch of Stripers with his neighbors. On one such memorable occasion, he gave me his favorite recipe for baking the fillets.

2 pounds striped bass fillets
    Salt and pepper
1 large onion,
    sliced into thin rings
2 teaspoons sweet basil
2 cups California Sauterne or
    other White Table Wine
2 teaspoons Worcestershire
    sauce
3 tablespoons butter
2 tomatoes, sliced
½ green pepper, sliced

Sprinkle fish fillets with salt and pepper. Lay fillets in oven-proof baking dish. Cover with onion rings. Sprinkle with basil. Pour on wine and Worcestershire sauce and allow to marinate several hours or over night. If the wine does not cover the fillets, turn them occasionally. Preheat oven to 375°. Dot fish with butter, distribute tomatoes and green pepper over and around fish. Bake 35 minutes or until fish flakes when tested with fork. Baste frequently with wine mixture in baking dish. Do not overcook.

My choice of wine to accompany this dish:
CALIFORNIA RIESLING, PINOT CHARDONNAY *or* **DRY SEMILLON**

Shellfish Thermidor

(4 SERVINGS)

Miss Margaret Shahenian, Guild Wine Company, San Francisco
With this rich dish, I serve plain boiled rice, sliced tomato salad with wine vinegar and oil dressing, and for dessert, pineapple sherbet with a sugar cookie.

4 tablespoons chopped onion
1 cup fresh mushrooms, sliced
¼ cup butter
¼ cup sifted flour
½ teaspoon salt
¼ teaspoon pepper
¼ teaspoon paprika
1 cup light cream
1 cup chicken broth
1 teaspoon Worcestershire
   sauce
1 egg yolk, beaten
¼ cup California Dry Sherry
2 lobster tails, cooked
1 pound prawns,
   cooked and cleaned
1 pound crab meat
   Fine dry bread crumbs

Preheat oven to 450°. Sauté onion and mushrooms in butter. Blend in flour and seasonings. Cook over low heat until bubbly. Remove from heat and stir in cream, chicken broth, Worcestershire sauce. Bring sauce to boil, stir in egg yolk, Sherry and prepared shellfish. Place mixture in shells or baking dish. Sprinkle with fine bread crumbs. Bake 5 minutes or until topping is brown.

 My choice of wine to accompany this dish: **CALIFORNIA SAUTERNE**

Crab Pie with Almonds

(6 TO 8 SERVINGS)

Mrs. E. A. Kirkman, Jr., Wente Bros., Livermore
I suggest that this be served as the fish course at dinner or as an entree for a luncheon. The recipe started when I tried to persuade a homemaking class of girls to make a Quiche Lorraine. They didn't like the idea at all, but when I presented them with this recipe, without the wine, they were delighted. That was my incentive to further develop this recipe with the addition of wine.

PASTRY
1 cup sifted flour
½ teaspoon salt
½ cup shortening
2 tablespoons California
   White Table Wine

FILLING
1 (7½-oz.) can crab meat
½ cup California
   White Table Wine
1 cup shredded Swiss cheese
1 green onion with tops,
   chopped
3 eggs, beaten slightly
¾ cup light cream
½ teaspoon salt
   Dash mace
½ cup sliced almonds

Pastry: Combine flour, salt, shortening, wine as for a regular pie crust, and roll very thin, then place in an 8-inch glass pie plate. Bake in a hot oven, 425°, for 5 minutes to insure a crisp crust. **Filling:** Marinate the crab in the wine at least 2 hours. When ready to prepare, sprinkle the shredded cheese into the partially baked pie crust. Drain wine from crab and set aside. Spread crab over cheese, sprinkle on onion. Combine eggs, cream, reserved wine, salt and mace and pour into pie shell. Sprinkle almonds on top. Bake at 325° for 45 minutes. Serve warm.

 My choice of wine to accompany this dish: **CALIFORNIA GREY RIESLING**

Wine Marinated Cracked Crab

(4 SERVINGS)

Mr. Vernon L. Singleton, University of California, Dept. Viticulture and Enology, Davis

2 medium-size Dungeness
    crabs
½ cup California
    Dry White Table Wine
½ cup lemon juice
½ cup salad oil
¾ teaspoon dry mustard
1 teaspoon salt
⅛ teaspoon pepper
1 small clove garlic,
    finely grated
1 egg

If possible have crabs cleaned and cracked at the market. You may need to recrack any difficult spots to make easy eating. Combine all ingredients except egg and crab in a bowl and mix well. Add egg and mix with a fork until well blended. Add cracked crab. Marinate in a covered bowl in refrigerator for at least 1 hour, mixing several times. Serve cracked crab with a little container of marinade and small forks or picks. An added touch is a small hot terry cloth rolled with a sprig of fresh mint to wipe the fingers.

My choice of wine to accompany this dish:
CALIFORNIA WHITE RIESLING *or* **CHARDONNAY**

Old Rancho Shrimp Creole

(6 SERVINGS)

Mrs. Joseph A. Filippi, Jr., Thomas Vineyards, Cucamonga

3 quarts water
2 teaspoons cooking oil
3 teaspoons salt
40 medium shrimp (2 to 2¼ lbs.)
½ cup butter or olive oil
1 medium onion, diced
2 cloves garlic, minced
1 medium green pepper, diced
3 stalks celery, diced
1 bay leaf
1 (8-oz.) can tomato sauce
½ cup water
½ cup California Sauterne
1 teaspoon salt

In large pan, boil water. Add oil and salt. Devein and clean shrimp. Let drain and drop into boiling water for only 5 minutes or until they turn pink. Drain and place on paper towel to dry. In large skillet or deep roasting pan, sauté in butter, onion, garlic, green pepper, celery and bay leaf for 5 minutes. Add tomato sauce, water, wine and salt. Simmer for 10 minutes. Add one shrimp at a time until all are in pan. Bake in a moderate oven (350°) 45 minutes or until sauce thickens and coats shrimp. There should be enough sauce left to serve over rice.

My choice of wine to accompany this dish:
CALIFORNIA SAUTERNE *or* **CHABLIS**

Crab Omelette Supreme

(3 SERVINGS)

Mrs. Sam J. Sebastiani, Samuele Sebastiani Winery, Sonoma

6 eggs
3 tablespoons California
    Dry Sherry
1½ cups finely chopped fresh
    Alaskan King Crab or
    1 (7½-oz.) can crabmeat
Dash of salt
¼ cup cream
½ teaspoon minced parsley
1 tablespoon butter

Separate egg whites from yolks. Beat egg whites until stiff. Add wine, salt and cream to yolks and beat until smooth. Fold yolks into stiffly beaten whites. Heat skillet over low flame, until hot but not smoking. Add butter, tip skillet back and forth until butter spreads evenly. Add combined egg mixture to skillet and spread evenly with fork. When omelette is slightly cooked but not firm, spread crabmeat mixed with parsley over center. Fold omelette and slide onto heated platter. Brush top with melted butter, place in preheated oven, 250°, for 15 minutes and serve immediately.

My choice of wine to accompany this dish:
CALIFORNIA GREEN HUNGARIAN

Skewered Shrimp In White Wine

(4 SERVINGS)

Mrs. George Pentek, The Christian Brothers, Fresno
Editor's note: This is a light and flavorful dish for lunch or supper
and it is very good with risotto.

20 raw jumbo shrimp
Canadian bacon or prosciutto,
   in wafer thin slices
3 tablespoons salad oil
1 tablespoon California Brandy
¼ cup light cream
¼ cup California
   Dry White Table Wine
⅓ cup consomme
2 teaspoons minced parsley
2 teaspoons lemon juice
½ teaspoon Worcestershire
   sauce
Dash cayenne pepper
Salt to taste

Shell and devein shrimp, leaving tail intact. Rinse and pat dry on paper towels. On each of 4 skewers thread 5 shrimp alternately with small squares of bacon or ham, piercing shrimp so flat sides lie flat in pan, brown lightly in hot salad oil on each side. Sprinkle with Brandy; add rest of ingredients. Cover lightly; simmer gently about 10 minutes. Remove to warm plates. Pour sauce over shrimp.

 My choice of wine to accompany this dish: **CALIFORNIA RIESLING**

Shrimp Tiffany

(4 SERVINGS)

Mrs. Maury Baldwin, Owens-Illinois Glass Co., Sacramento
My very dear friend, Grace Tiffany, who also happens to be my husband's girl Friday, gave me this recipe. We know good food and good wine keep him happy. This is excellent for large groups. Prepare almost completely a day or two ahead of time. At the last moment, add sour cream, blend and heat. Serve in chafing dishes. Very colorful, especially if sprinkled with finely chopped parsley.

1 (10-oz.) can frozen
   shrimp soup
2 tablespoons chopped onion
½ cup sliced fresh
   or canned mushrooms
2 tablespoons butter
1 tablespoon flour
⅓ cup California Dry Sherry
1 cup dairy sour cream
Dash pepper
1 pound medium-size fresh,
   cooked prawns

Thaw frozen shrimp soup. Sauté onions and mushrooms in butter. Add flour and blend. Add soup, Sherry (and liquid, if canned mushrooms used) and cook until thick. Add sour cream, pepper and prawns which have been deveined and cut into halves or quarters.

 My choice of wine to accompany this dish:
CALIFORNIA PINOT CHARDONNAY

Scallops in Wine Cream Sauce

(6 SERVINGS)

Miss Gyl Rheingans, Sanger Winery Association, Sanger
Editor's note: Scallops in a wine-cream sauce, embellished with mushrooms and bacon bits are usually served with (or over) rice.

2 pounds sea scallops,
    fresh or frozen
8 slices bacon, diced
2 tablespoons butter
    or margarine
2 tablespoons minced onion
3 tablespoons finely diced
    green peppers
¼ cup flour
¾ cup chicken broth
1 cup light cream
1 (3-oz.) can sliced broiled
    mushrooms
½ teaspoon salt
    Pepper
3 tablespoons California
    Marsala
    Chopped parsley

Defrost scallops, if frozen; cut in half, crosswise, cover with boiling water, simmer 5 to 7 minutes or until tender; drain. Cook bacon until crisp, drain. Return 2 tablespoons bacon drippings to skillet, add butter, onion and green pepper. Cook until vegetables are soft but not brown. Blend in flour. Add broth, cream and liquid from mushrooms; stir until thickened. Add mushrooms, scallops, salt, pepper and wine. Heat to serving temperature. Sprinkle crisp bacon bits and parsley on top.

My choice of wine to accompany this dish:
CALIFORNIA JOHANNISBERG RIESLING

Sherry and Parmesan Scampi

(2 SERVINGS)

Mrs. D. C. Turrentine, Wine Advisory Board, San Francisco
This recipe is much easier and better than others I have tried for scampi.
I serve it with fresh French bread and green salad.

½ cup butter or margarine
1 clove garlic, crushed
2 teaspoons Worcestershire
    sauce
    Juice of ½ lemon
¼ cup California Dry Sherry
1 teaspoon sugar
2 teaspoons fresh dill, chopped
1 pound raw shrimp,
    shelled and deveined
¼ cup minced parsley
2 cups hot cooked rice
    Parmesan cheese

In shallow pan, melt butter over low heat. Add next 6 ingredients; mix well. Arrange shrimp in a single layer in the sauce. Spoon sauce over shrimp. Broil at low heat 8 minutes. Remove from broiler. Let stand for 15 minutes. Sprinkle on parsley. Broil at high heat for 3 minutes. Spoon sauce over rice. Sprinkle with Parmesan cheese. Arrange shrimp over rice.

My choice of wine to accompany this dish:
CALIFORNIA CHABLIS *or other* **DRY WHITE TABLE WINE**

Specialty Main Dishes

Eggs à la Monsignor Gerald Cox

(4 SERVINGS)

Mrs. Edmund A. Rossi, Jr., Italian Swiss Colony, Asti
This was served to us for brunch by our good friend, Monsignor Gerald Cox of Sonoma County.
He prepared this delicious dish and served it with hot buttered rolls and a chilled bottle of
champagne. It is easy to make but yummy! Our whole family thought it was terrific.

1 dozen eggs
¼ cup California Dry
    White Table Wine
1 or 2 bell peppers,
    seeded and chopped
½ pound fresh mushrooms,
    sliced
3 or 4 green onions, chopped
¼ cup oil or butter
3 or 4 Italian sausages,
    cut in bite-size pieces
2 tablespoons oil or butter
    Salt and pepper

Beat eggs with fork, add wine, set aside. Sauté all three vegetables in ¼ cup oil or butter until tender. In a separate frying pan, sauté sausage for 10 to 15 minutes. Drain off all grease and remove sausage. Over medium heat add 2 tablespoons oil or butter to pan, pour in eggs. As they start to set, add all other ingredients. Stir constantly until eggs are cooked to desired consistency.

My choice of wine to accompany this dish: **CALIFORNIA CHAMPAGNE**

Regina Fritata

(6 SERVINGS)

Mrs. John B. Ellena, Regina Grape Products Co., Etiwanda
This recipe may be used as a meat substitute, considering the amount of cheese and the
number of eggs in it. However, I believe, it is best served with a light meat
such as lamb roast or chicken. It's also good with a spaghetti dinner.

1 (10-oz.) package frozen
    chopped spinach
1 medium onion,
    finely chopped
2 tablespoons butter or
    margarine
8 eggs
⅓ cup California Dry Sherry
¼ teaspoon salt
¼ teaspoon pepper
    Dash of powdered rosemary
    Pinch of sweet basil leaves
1 cup Parmesan cheese

Cook spinach as directed on package. Drain well, pressing out as much liquid as possible. Sauté onion in butter or margarine until golden brown. Beat eggs in mixing bowl and add all ingredients except ¼ cup cheese and mix well. Pour mixture into an 8 x 12-inch greased baking dish. Sprinkle ¼ cup Parmesan cheese over top. Bake at 325° for 25 minutes, then place under broiler for 5 minutes to get top golden brown.

My choice of wine to accompany this dish: **CALIFORNIA ROSÉ**

Fisherman's Soup

(8 TO 10 SERVINGS)

Mrs. Robert Diana, Villa Armando, Pleasanton
If you like variety in your seafood, this is your dish. For any of the fish mentioned you can substitute any others you may prefer. But do not use crab meat, it tends to disintegrate and loses its flavor unless left in the shell.

½ pound red snapper
½ pound bass
½ pound halibut
½ pound cod
12 cherrystone clams in shell
1 pound jumbo shrimp
1 cup flour
3 beaten eggs
½ cup bread crumbs
½ cup olive oil
½ cup butter
3 firm tomatoes, sliced thin
3 cloves garlic, mashed
12 sprigs parsley
½ teaspoon crushed red pepper
½ teaspoon black pepper
1 teaspoon salt
2 bay leaves crumbled
2 cups California Dry
    White Table Wine
2 cups boiling water
2 loaves Italian bread

Cut the 4 kinds of fish into 2-inch pieces. Do not open the clams. Wash them under cold running water and scrub with a vegetable brush. Discard any open ones. Shell shrimp, wash and devein them while still raw. Split down middle lengthwise. Sprinkle fish with flour then dip into beaten eggs. Roll in bread crumbs. Place 6 tablespoons of oil in a skillet and heat. Sauté fish pieces on each side for 5 minutes. Remove skillet from heat. Place butter and remaining oil in bottom of large soup pot. Heat, add shrimp, clams in shell and sliced tomatoes. Cover and cook 10 minutes. Chop mashed garlic and parsley together and add to soup with red and black pepper, salt and bay leaf. Add sautéed fish and pour in oil and juices from skillet. Add wine. Cover and cook 5 minutes. Add boiling water and cook another 10 minutes uncovered. Turn off heat but keep pot covered. Slice bread and toast in oven. Place 2 slices of toast in each large soup plate. On this arrange pieces of fish, then clams and shrimp, then the juice.

My choice of wine to accompany this dish: **CALIFORNIA DRY MUSCAT**

Risotto Italiene

(5 SERVINGS)

Mrs. Aldo Nerelli, Pesenti Winery, Templeton
An exciting change from potatoes, this risotto is a good accompaniment with any type of meat.
Editor's note: This cheese and rice specialty is also hearty enough to serve as a main dish at a luncheon or family supper.

¼ cup butter
½ cup finely cut onions
1 clove garlic, thinly sliced
1 (2-oz.) can mushrooms
1 cup long grain rice, uncooked
2 tablespoons chopped parsley
Salt and pepper
3 to 4 cups beef broth from
    boiled meat
¾ cup California
    Dry White Wine
⅛ teaspoon saffron
½ cup Parmesan cheese, grated
½ cup Cheddar cheese, grated

Melt butter, add onions, garlic, drained mushrooms, and sauté until light brown. Add rice, parsley and salt and continue cooking until brown. Add hot broth, wine and saffron, a little at a time, until rice becomes tender. Continue cooking over medium heat. When rice is cooked stir in cheese and heat gently just until cheeses melt.

My choice of wine to accompany this dish:
CALIFORNIA ZINFANDEL *or* **PINOT NOIR**

Rice with Mushrooms

(6 SERVINGS)

Mrs. Robert Weaver, University of California, Dept. Viticulture and Enology, Davis

1 cup raw regular rice,
    uncooked
1 cup chopped tomatoes
1 pound mushrooms, sliced
½ cup chopped onion
½ cup butter
3 cups chicken broth
½ cup California
    Red Table Wine
2 teaspoons salt
⅛ teaspoon pepper
1 cup cooked green peas
¼ cup grated Parmesan cheese

In a large skillet, cook rice, tomatoes, mushrooms and onion in butter for about 10 minutes, stirring occasionally. Add broth, wine and seasonings; mix well. Cover. Simmer for about 45 minutes, or until rice is tender and liquid is absorbed. Stir in peas. Heat until peas are warmed through. Sprinkle with Parmesan cheese. Serve.

My choice of wine to accompany this dish:
CALIFORNIA CABERNET, PINOT NOIR, *or* **ZINFANDEL**

Omelet with Artichokes

(1 SERVING)

Mrs. William Bonetti, Charles Krug Winery, St. Helena

OMELET
2 eggs
2 tablespoons cream
Salt
3 canned artichoke hearts,
    sliced very thin
1 tablespoon butter
CHEESE SAUCE
½ cup shredded cheese
    (fontina or similar)
1 teaspoon cornstarch
3 tablespoons California
    Chablis

Omelet: Beat eggs, cream and salt together with a fork until well blended. Mix with artichokes. In a skillet heat the butter until golden; pour in the egg mixture and tilt the skillet until the bottom is covered. Cook to desired consistency. **Sauce:** Coat the cheese with cornstarch; heat wine in heavy saucepan until it bubbles; turn heat to simmer; add the cheese, stirring constantly until melted. To serve, slide omelet onto a preheated plate; pour the sauce over it and fold in half; serve immediately.

My choice of wine to accompany this dish:
CALIFORNIA JOHANNISBERG RIESLING

Valley Royal Eggs

(12 SERVINGS)

Mr. Joseph J. Franzia, Franzia Brothers Winery, Ripon

12 egg yolks
    Boiling water
1¾ cups sugar
2½ cups water
1 (3-inch) cinnamon stick,
    broken into small pieces
⅓ cup California Sherry

Preheat oven to 350°. Butter bottom and sides of a 9″ x 5″ loaf pan. In small bowl of electric mixer, at medium speed, beat egg yolks until very thick and lemon-colored, about 7 minutes. Pour into prepared pan. Place loaf pan in shallow baking pan. Pour boiling water to 1-inch depth around loaf pan. Bake 20 minutes or until cake tester inserted in center comes out clean. Remove to wire rack, and let cool in pan. In medium saucepan, combine sugar, water and cinnamon stick. Bring to a boil, stirring until sugar is dissolved. Boil 5 minutes. Cut cooled egg mixture into 12 even-sized serving pieces. Put a piece of cinnamon stick from syrup in each. Turn cubes into syrup; simmer gently, uncovered, 10 minutes. Remove from heat, stir in Sherry. Cool, then refrigerate, covered, at least 24 hours.

 My choice of wine to accompany this dish: **CALIFORNIA CHAMPAGNE**

Moussaka Tsapralis

(10 TO 12 SERVINGS)

Mrs. Don Rudolph, Cresta Blanca Wine Company, Livermore
This recipe was given to me by Cleo Tsapralis, an excellent cook.

1 eggplant
½ cup shortening
2 tablespoons butter
4 medium onions, thinly sliced
3 cloves garlic, chopped
1½ pounds ground beef
1 teaspoon salt
½ teaspoon thyme
½ teaspoon oregano
½ cup canned tomatoes
½ cup California
    White Table Wine
2 egg whites, slightly beaten
½ cup bread crumbs
    SAUCE
2 tablespoons butter
2 tablespoons flour
1½ cups milk
½ teaspoon salt
2 egg yolks, slightly beaten
⅛ teaspoon nutmeg

Cut unpeeled eggplant in lengthwise slices, fry in shortening until brown then transfer to platter lined with absorbent paper. Melt butter and add sliced onions and chopped garlic, fry until limp, add ground beef, salt, thyme, oregano, tomatoes and wine, cook slowly for 30 minutes. Cool, mix in egg whites and half bread crumbs. While mixture cooks, make sauce. **Sauce:** Melt butter. Stir in flour, add milk and salt, stir until thick. Add egg yolks to sauce, stir until blended well, add nutmeg. Butter large casserole, cover bottom with remaining bread crumbs, arrange a layer of eggplant, then a layer of meat mixture, repeat layers then cover with sauce. Bake uncovered at 350° for 1 hour.

My choice of wine to accompany this dish:
ANY CALIFORNIA RED TABLE WINE

Shell Macaroni in Curried Clam Sauce

(4 TO 6 SERVINGS)

Mr. and Mrs. Ferrer Filipello, Italian Swiss Colony, Asti

5 tablespoons butter
1 (8-oz.) can sliced mushrooms,
    drained
1 (7-oz.) can minced clams,
    drained, save liquid
¼ teaspoon monosodium
    glutamate
½ teaspoon salt
½ cup California Vermouth
1 teaspoon curry powder
    Pinch cayenne pepper
1 tablespoon oyster sauce
    (may be purchased at a
    Chinese grocery)
½ cup grated dry Monterey
    cheese
½ cup grated Cheddar cheese
1 tablespoon parsley, chopped
1 tablespoon chives, chopped
1 (12-oz.) package
    large shell macaroni
    Water
    Salt

Melt butter in skillet over low heat. Add drained mushrooms and sauté for 3 minutes with occasional stirring. Add drained minced clams, monosodium glutamate, salt and stir. Add clam liquid and Vermouth and allow to simmer. Add curry, cayenne and oyster sauce. Stir in cheese, parsley and chives. If sauce becomes too sticky, stir in more Vermouth. Cook macaroni in salted boiling water for 15 to 20 minutes until cooked but not mushy soft. Drain well and mix with sauce.

My choice of wine to accompany this dish:
CALIFORNIA PINOT BLANC or CHAMPAGNE

This section provides the accents to a meal — the soups, the salads, and the vegetables. If the main dish is the star of an Epicurean presentation, then these accompaniments are the supporting players. They have strength but not obtrusiveness. They don't compete with the main dish, they complement it.

ACCOMPANIMENTS TO MAIN DISHES

Vegetables

Bear Mountain Zucchini

(4 TO 6 BIG SERVINGS)

Mrs. Hector Castro, Bear Mountain Winery, Di Giorgio
One year I grew zucchini and having more than we or the whole neighborhood could use,
I asked all my friends for their recipes for using zucchini. This recipe evolved from three
recipes and this is the first time I've even written it down. It is now one of our family favorites.

1½ pounds zucchini, sliced
3 tablespoons cooking oil
2 tablespoons olive oil
1 (8-oz.) can tomato sauce
1 clove garlic, chopped
Dash sweet basil
½ cup California
Red Table Wine
¼ pound Jack cheese, sliced
3 tablespoons grated
Parmesan cheese

Fry zucchini in oil and drain. In same pan (drain off excess oil), combine olive oil, tomato sauce, garlic, basil and wine and cook until thickened. In greased, 2-quart baking dish, put zucchini, sauce and cheese slices in layers. Pour remaining sauce over top and sprinkle with Parmesan cheese. Bake at 350° 30 to 40 minutes or until it bubbles.

My choice of wine to accompany this dish:
either **CALIFORNIA RED** *or* **WHITE TABLE WINE,**
depending on the main dish.

Scalloped Onions

(6 TO 8 SERVINGS)

Mrs. Joseph Concannon, Jr., Concannon Vineyard, Livermore
This recipe is a cinch to prepare. It can be done well ahead of time and the results are superb.
It is an excellent accompaniment for baked ham.

3 tablespoons butter or
margarine
3 tablespoons flour
1 cup canned consomme
¼ cup California Dry Sherry
¼ cup grated Parmesan cheese
2 tablespoons chopped parsley
Salt, pepper
2 (1-lb.) cans small whole
onions, drained
¼ cup fine dry bread crumbs
mixed
2 teaspoons melted butter

Melt butter and stir in flour; add consomme and Sherry; cook, stirring constantly, until mixture boils and thickens. Add cheese, parsley, salt and pepper. Combine this sauce with the onions. Turn into a greased casserole. Mix bread crumbs with melted butter and sprinkle on top. Bake in moderate oven (350°–375°) for about 25 minutes.

My choice of wine to accompany this dish:
CALIFORNIA JOHANNISBERG RIESLING *or* **MOSELLE**

Fresh Broccoli with Cream Cheese Sauce

(6 TO 8 SERVINGS)

Mrs. Peter Mirassou, Mirassou Vineyards, San Jose
This recipe was given to me by a good friend whose family is a large producer of broccoli
in the Salinas Valley. This is one of her favorite ways of serving it.

2 pounds broccoli
2 teaspoons salt
4 tablespoons butter (½ cube)
4 tablespoons flour
1 cup cream
1 bouillon cube
¾ cup hot water
2 tablespoons California
  Dry Sherry
2 tablespoons lemon juice
  Pepper
½ teaspoon monosodium
  glutamate
¼ cup grated Parmesan cheese
½ cup grated Cheddar cheese
¼ cup slivered almonds

Separate broccoli and wash. Then cook with small amount of water until barely tender. Drain. Arrange in shallow baking dish. While broccoli is cooking, melt butter and blend in flour. Pour in cream and bouillon cube, dissolved first in the hot water. Stirring, cook until smooth and thickened. Add Sherry, lemon juice, pepper and monosodium glutamate. Pour sauce over broccoli. Sprinkle grated cheeses and almonds over top. Bake 20 minutes or until hot.

My choice of wine to accompany this dish: Any wine that would complement whatever meat is served with the broccoli; perhaps **CALIFORNIA ZINFANDEL** *if a red meat or* **CHENIN BLANC** *if poultry.*

Egg Plant Parmigiana

(8 SERVINGS)

Mrs. Leon A. Kirschenmann, East-Side Winery, Lodi
I have discovered that people who think they don't care for egg plant really go for this.
Editor's note: This dish is rich enough to serve as a main dish,
accompanied by a tossed green salad.

EGG PLANT
1 large egg plant,
  sliced in ¼-inch slices
1 egg
  Flour
  Oil
TOMATO SAUCE
1 large onion, chopped
2 tablespoons oil
1 (1 lb. 12-oz.) can whole
  plum tomatoes
¾ cup California Marsala
½ (1½-oz.) package spaghetti
  sauce mix
1 teaspoon instant minced
  garlic
  Salt and pepper
2 cups fresh bread crumbs
1½ cups grated Monterey Jack
  cheese
2 tablespoons dry or fresh
  chopped parsley

Egg Plant: Dip slices of egg plant in slightly beaten egg. Roll in flour and brown in oil on both sides. Set aside while preparing tomato sauce. **Tomato Sauce:** Sauté 1 large onion in oil in pan in which you browned egg plant. When onion is soft add tomatoes, wine, spaghetti sauce mix, minced garlic, and salt and pepper. Simmer mixture until thick. Toss together bread crumbs, 1 cup grated cheese and parsley. Arrange layer of egg plant slices in 9 x 13″ flat baking pan. Sprinkle ½ crumb mixture over slices, pour ½ tomato sauce over crumb layer. Repeat process and sprinkle top with remaining ½ cup grated cheese. Bake at 350° until heated through.

My choice of wine to accompany this dish: **CALIFORNIA RUBY CABERNET** *or* **EMERALD RIESLING** *or* **CHENIN BLANC**

Sherried String Beans

(8 SERVINGS)

Mrs. Jack H. Farrior, Jr., Almaden Vineyards, Los Gatos
Editor's note: This vegetable casserole dish with the delicate Sherry flavor
is an excellent accompaniment for baked ham, hot or cold.

2 (10 to 12-oz.) packages frozen,
  French-style string beans
½ cup California Dry Sherry
1 (1-lb.) can whole onions
1 (10½-oz.) can mushroom soup
½ teaspoon nutmeg
¼ teaspoon salt
⅓ cup slivered almonds

Cook string beans according to directions on package. Drain and add Sherry, onions, mushroom soup, nutmeg, salt and almonds. Place in baking dish and bake at 350° for ½ hour.

Editor's note: If this dish is served with ham,
CALIFORNIA ROSÉ *is the ideal accompanying wine.*

Le Celeri à la Eschscholtzia

(6 SERVINGS)

Dr. Salvatore P. Lucia, University of California, School of Medicine, San Francisco
Editor's note: Braised celery with wine and caraway flavorings is an unusual vegetable accompaniment for slices of cold roast beef or tongue. The short simmering period is important, because the celery is already cooked, and longer heating will make it less attractive.

12 canned celery hearts
   with juice
¼ cup butter
   Juice of 1 lemon
½ cup California Sherry
1 teaspoon whole caraway seed

Drain celery, reserving liquid. Braise celery in butter in a covered frying pan. Then add half of the juice in which the celery was canned. When thoroughly heated, add lemon juice, Sherry and sprinkle caraway seed evenly over celery. Replace cover on pan and simmer slowly for 3 to 5 minutes. Serve immediately on warmed plates.

 My choice of wine to serve with this dish: **CALIFORNIA CHARDONNAY**

Broccoli Crown

(8 TO 10 SERVINGS)

Mrs. Paul L. Halpern, United Vintners, Madera
This is a very tasty dish. I serve it with a prime rib roast menu or butterfly leg of lamb.

1 bunch broccoli
   (1¼ to 1½ pounds)
1 small onion, chopped
4 tablespoons butter
4 tablespoons flour
1 teaspoon seasoned salt
½ cup grated Parmesan cheese
3 eggs
1 cup milk
½ cup mayonnaise
¼ cup chopped parsley
3 tablespoons California
   Dry Sherry

Trim outer leaves and tough ends and peel stems. Chop flowers and stems in ½-inch slices. Cook in small amount of boiling salted water 10 minutes. Drain. Sauté onion in butter until soft. Stir in flour and salt. Cook stirring constantly until bubbly. Stir in milk and continue stirring until it thickens and boils one minute. Beat eggs slightly and stir in ½ cup of the heated sauce. Then stir egg mixture back quickly into remaining sauce. Cook, stirring constantly until mixture thickens again. Remove from heat. Stir in mayonnaise, Sherry and parsley. Fold in broccoli. Spoon into a well-greased 3-quart ring mold and sprinkle on Parmesan cheese. Bake for 30 minutes or until set at 350°. Let ring stand several minutes. Loosen with knife and invert onto serving plate.

Editor's note: **CALIFORNIA BURGUNDY** *is good with prime rib roast and* **ROSÉ** *is good with leg of lamb.*

63

Artichoke Hearts in Wine

(4 TO 6 SERVINGS)

Mrs. Sam J. Sebastiani, Samule Sebastiani Winery, Sonoma
This recipe originated among families who lived in the artichoke center of the world,
the Castroville area of California. It is a food that many have never tasted,
but so far all new-comers that I have served this to have really enjoyed it.

12 small artichokes
½ cup olive oil
½ cup California
    Dry White Table Wine
2 cloves garlic,
    minced or mashed
½ teaspoon salt
    Dash of pepper and garlic salt

Cut slice off top of each artichoke, then cook artichokes in boiling salted water for 25 minutes, or until almost tender; drain. Pull off all tough outer leaves, and cut off stem so that only the hearts of the artichokes remain. Cut hearts in half lengthwise and scrape out choke. Combine olive oil and wine in a heavy saucepan with a tight fitting cover. Add pepper, garlic salt and artichoke hearts. Cover and simmer, turning occasionally, for 20 to 30 minutes or until artichokes are thoroughly done. Add a little more wine and oil if the sauce gets dry.

My choice of wine to accompany this dish:
CALIFORNIA RED *or* **WHITE TABLE WINE,**
depending on the complete meal.

Madeira Onion Rings

(4 SERVINGS)

Mrs. N. C. Mirassou, Mirassou Vineyards, San Jose
Editor's note: These glazed onion rings make an interesting change from the creamed onions
served with most turkey or roast beef. They'll also add distinction to meat loaf or hamburgers.

4 tablespoons butter
4 large onions,
    sliced ¼-inch thick
    and separated into rings
⅔ cup California Madeira
1 tablespoon chopped parsley
    Salt and pepper

Melt butter in heavy skillet. Toss onions in the hot butter, but do not sauté long enough to make onions soft. Add ½ cup of wine; cover pan. Raise heat and let onions cook over a medium flame until they are tender. Remove cover and let the wine reduce to a glaze in the pan. Stir in the remaining Madeira and chopped parsley.

Editor's note: Serve a **CALIFORNIA RED** *or* **WHITE TABLE WINE**
depending on the main dish of the meal.

Green Peppers Florentine

(8 SERVINGS)

Mrs. Jack H. Farrior, Jr., Almaden Vineyards, Los Gatos
This is our favorite vegetable to serve with Mandarin Pheasant. Editor's note: (see page 41).

6 green peppers
2 tablespoons olive oil
1 tablespoon wine vinegar
½ teaspoon sugar
3 tablespoons capers
2 tablespoons chopped olives
¼ teaspoon oregano
½ cup California Sauterne

Slice green peppers lengthwise, sauté until limp in olive oil. Add wine vinegar, sugar, capers, chopped olives, oregano and Sauterne. Simmer 20 minutes.

 My choice of wine to accompany this dish: **CALIFORNIA SAUTERNE**

Canneloni with Spinach Souffle Filling

(8 TO 10 SERVINGS)

Mrs. Louis P. Martini, Louis M. Martini Winery, St. Helena
This dish may be prepared 3 or 4 hours ahead of time and refrigerated.
I serve it as a first course, for luncheon or for a buffet.

VELOUTE SAUCE
2 cups canned chicken broth
3 tablespoons each, sliced
    onion, carrot, celery
½ cup California
    Sauterne or Vermouth
3 sprigs parsley
1 bay leaf
    Pinch of thyme
2 tablespoons butter
3 tablespoons flour
SPINACH FILLING
2 (10-oz.) packages spinach
    frozen in butter sauce,
    partially thawed
2 tablespoons arrowroot powder
2 cups ricotta cheese
2 eggs
2 tablespoons grated
    Parmesan cheese
¼ teaspoon nutmeg
½ teaspoon celery salt
¼ teaspoon garlic salt
20 crepes (see page 85)
    Swiss or Gruyere cheese,
    grated

Veloute sauce: Simmer broth, onion, carrot, celery, wine, parsley, bay leaf, thyme together about 30 minutes; taste and strain. Bring stock back to boiling point. In heavy-bottomed pan, melt butter and work in flour stirring constantly until flour is cooked but not browned. Add stock, stirring vigorously with a wire whip until the sauce is thickened. **Filling:** Cook spinach. When cooked and still hot, drain and put in blender and blend in arrowroot. Place spinach in large mixing bowl. In blender place ricotta cheese, eggs, Parmesan cheese, nutmeg, celery salt and garlic salt. Blend and mix with spinach mixture. Spread not more than half of the Veloute sauce in the bottom of a flat square baking dish. Holding crepe in palm of one hand, spoon filling down center, fold over ends and place with lapped-over portion face down in baking dish. Spread over with remaining sauce. Sprinkle generously with shredded Swiss or Gruyere cheese. When ready to serve, heat in a hot (400°) oven for 20 minutes. Cheese should be melted, sauce bubbling. It may be browned for a minute under the broiler.

My choice of wine to accompany this dish:
CALIFORNIA DRY SEMILLON

Green Beans Française

(6 SERVINGS)

Mrs. Alessandro Baccari, Baccari Wine Festival, San Francisco

1 pound green beans,
    cut French style
⅓ cube butter
2 tablespoons olive oil
1 large clove garlic,
    cut in 3 sections
4 slices lemon
1 drop Worcestershire sauce
⅓ cup toasted slivered almonds
½ teaspoon salt
⅛ teaspoon pepper
1 tablespoon chopped
    minced parsley
½ cup California Dry Sherry
½ cup California Dry Sauterne

Boil green beans until tender (do not over-cook). Set aside. Melt butter and oil together; add garlic, lemon, almonds, Worcestershire sauce, salt and pepper and sauté slowly on very low fire; stir with fork, making sure not to break up garlic; press on lemon slices to remove juice. Add parsley, Sherry and Sauterne and cook slowly for about 25 minutes. Remove garlic and lemon, add green beans and simmer 10 to 12 minutes longer. If sauce gets too thick, add more wine.

Editor's note: If this dish is served with roast beef, **CALIFORNIA PINOT NOIR** *or* **CABERNET SAUVIGNON** *is a good choice as the accompanying wine.*

Soups and Salads

Charbonnet Soup Supreme

(6 SERVINGS)

Mrs. Edmund G. Carbone, Carbone Napa Valley Winery, Napa
I made this recipe up. It's wonderful for the busy woman as it serves as a main course.
This is a rich soup, almost a meal itself. One could serve Italian bread with garlic and a dash
of Parmesan cheese mixed with butter to spread on the bread before heating it.
A light dessert such as a cheesecake would do the trick.

1 **pound chicken wings** 1 **cup water** 1 **cup California Burgundy** 1 **cup tomato juice** 1 **teaspoon salt** 10 **peppercorns** ¼ **cup butter** 1½ **cups finely chopped onion** 1½ **cups finely chopped celery** 2 **tablespoons flour** 1½ **cups light cream**	Cook chicken wings in water, wine and tomato juice with salt and peppercorns added. Cook until tender, 20 to 30 minutes. Cool. Remove meat from bones, discarding skin, and chop or cut meat in small pieces. There will be about ¾ cup. Strain peppercorns from broth and reserve broth. In a saucepan, heat butter, add onion and celery and sauté until tender, but not brown. Stir in flour, reserved chicken broth and cream. Bring to a boil, stirring constantly. Add diced chicken. Reheat before serving. This is great to make and freeze.

My choice of wine to accompany this dish: **CALIFORNIA DRY SHERRY**

Mushroom Cream Soup

(6 SERVINGS)

Mrs. Charles van Kriedt, California Wineletter, San Francisco

1 **pound fresh mushrooms** 1 **cup California** 　**White Table Wine** ¼ **cup California Dry Sherry** 1 **carrot** 1 **stalk celery with leaves** 1 **clove garlic** 1 **onion** 3 **tablespoons butter** 　**Parsley** 3 **tablespoons flour** 3 **cups milk, heated** 　**Pinch nutmeg** 　**Salt, pepper, monosodium** 　**glutamate to taste** 1 **cup cream**	Slice mushrooms into pan with a tight lid. Pour on wines and bring to a boil. Cover tightly and steam until mushrooms are soft, about 10 minutes. Drain mushrooms, reserving liquid, and puree them through a food mill or swirl a few seconds in a blender. Hold. Slice carrot, celery, garlic and onion. In another saucepan, melt butter and brown vegetables, adding a few sprigs of parsley. Now stir in flour and slowly add heated milk, stirring constantly to keep sauce smooth as it thickens. Add nutmeg, salt, pepper and monosodium glutamate to taste. Hold just under a boil for 10 minutes, then cool and strain out vegetables. Combine mushrooms, strained milk sauce and wine bouillon. Add cream and reheat, preferably in a double boiler, as the soup must not boil. Adjust seasoning and serve very hot, garnished with chopped parsley.

Editor's note: Serve **CALIFORNIA DRY SHERRY** *with this mushroom soup and you'll taste again how well these two flavors complement each other.*

Pink Strawberry Soup

(8 SERVINGS)

Mrs. Richard W. Wilson, Vie-Del Company, Fresno

1 cup fresh ripe strawberries,
    washed, hulled and sliced
4 cups California Port
1 cup water
¼ cup sugar
    Pinch of salt
3 tablespoons arrowroot
¼ cup water
    Hot cream

In a saucepan, mix strawberries, wine and water. Bring to boil. Stir in sugar and salt. Mix arrowroot with water, add a few spoonfuls of hot soup, then stir into hot soup. Cook stirring frequently until soup thickens. Chill. Serve cold, topped with hot cream. Frozen raspberries can also be used, omitting the sugar.

Editor's note: **CALIFORNIA ROSÉ** *or* **LIGHT SWEET MUSCAT** *would be good wine accompaniments for this fruit soup.*

Vichyssoise

(6 SERVINGS)

Mrs. George Al Berry, E. & J. Gallo Winery, Modesto
This makes an excellent first course followed by a green salad with Gourmet Dressing [see below] and Ernie's Tenderloin Brochette [see Page 22]. I usually serve this course in the living room before sitting down in the dining room. It simplifies the table-clearing process.

4 cups coarsely diced raw
    potatoes
½ cup finely chopped
    green onions
2½ cups chicken consomme
¼ cup crumbled blue cheese
½ teaspoon celery salt
½ cup California Riesling
2 cups light cream

Combine potatoes, green onions and chicken consomme in a saucepan; bring to a boil. Cover and cook until potatoes are tender, 10 to 15 minutes. Then put mixture in a blender, add the blue cheese and blend about 30 seconds. Add celery salt, wine and cream. Blend and chill thoroughly. Serve in soup cups with a sprinkling of minced chives.

My choice of wine to accompany this dish: **CALIFORNIA RIESLING**

Gourmet Salad Dressing

(2 CUPS)

Mrs. George Al Berry, E. & J. Gallo Winery, Modesto
This dressing over plain lettuce, can serve as the salad course for virtually any dinner menu. It also makes an excellent luncheon dish served on wedges of crisp lettuce with slices of tomato, whole shrimp, and cooked asparagus spears. Accompany with crisp rolls and glasses of the same California wine used in the dressing.

2 (3-oz.) package cream cheese
1 teaspoon grated onion
¼ teaspoon garlic salt
½ teaspoon salt
⅛ teaspoon paprika
¼ cup California
    Dry White Wine
½ cup dairy sour cream
2 tablespoons chili sauce
1 (7½-oz.) can undrained
    minced clams
¼ cup finely chopped
    green onions

Beat cheese until soft. Blend in grated onion, garlic salt, salt, paprika, and wine. Add remaining ingredients. Beat until well blended. Refrigerate until ready to use.

My choice of wine to accompany this dish:
CALIFORNIA DRY WHITE TABLE WINE

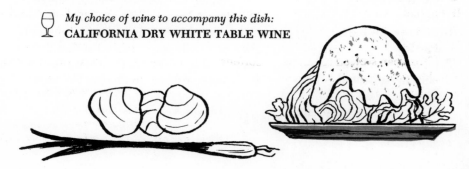

Tangy Tuna Mold

(4 TO 6 SERVINGS)

Mrs. Richard Peterson, Beaulieu Vineyard, Rutherford
Editor's note: This Sherry-flavored tuna mold is smooth and rich. Serve it as a main dish salad for luncheon or supper, accompanied by a dry white wine, chilled to a refreshingly cool temperature.

1 envelope unflavored gelatin
¼ cup California Sherry
1 cup dairy sour cream
2 tablespoons catsup
¾ teaspoon salt
½ cup finely chopped
    green pepper
½ cup finely chopped celery
1 (7-oz.) can drained tuna
2 tablespoons lemon juice
¼ cup chopped green onion

Soften gelatin in Sherry, dissolve over hot water. Combine with remaining ingredients, pour into mold and chill. Garnish with ripe olives and fresh parsley.

🍷 *Editor's note:* **CALIFORNIA RIESLING** *would enhance the flavor of this salad.*

Lentil Soup

(7 TO 8 CUPS)

Mrs. Clifton Chappell, Thomas Vineyards, Cucamonga

1¼ cups lentils
1 teaspoon salt
    Water (to cover)
½ cup California Burgundy
½ green pepper, diced
½ onion, diced
1 (16-oz.) can tomatoes or
    2 small (6-oz.) cans
    vegetable juice

Rinse lentils and cook covered in salted boiling water (at simmering) for about an hour. Add remainder of ingredients and simmer another hour or until lentils are tender.

🍷 *Editor's note: When presented as a dinner course,*
serve this soup with a glass of **CALIFORNIA DRY SHERRY.**

Tomato Aspic

(8 TO 10 SERVINGS)

Mrs. William B. Hewitt, U.C. San Joaquin Valley Research and Extension Center, Lodi
Editor's note: This is a light salad, delicately flavored with white wine.

2 envelopes unflavored gelatin
½ cup cold water
1 (8-oz.) can tomato sauce
½ cup water
1 (16-oz.) can stewed tomatoes
2 tablespoons chopped parsley
2 cups California
    Gewurztraminer

Soften gelatin in ½ cup cold water; set aside. Pour tomato sauce in saucepan, rinse can out with ½ cup water and add to tomato sauce. Mix in stewed tomatoes and parsley and bring mixture to boil. Strain into measuring cup. Reheat 1½ cups strained mixture to boiling point then stir in softened gelatin and wine. Pour into 2-quart mold or glass utility pan and refrigerate until firm. Serve on butter lettuce with a mayonnaise salad dressing thinned with Gewurztraminer wine.

🍷 *Editor's note: The same wine used in preparation,* **CALIFORNIA**
GEWURZTRAMINER, *would be a good choice for the accompanying beverage.*

69

Fruit Wine Compote

(6 TO 8 SERVINGS)

Christine Pedroncelli, J. Pedroncelli Winery, Geyserville
This salad makes a spectacular centerpiece when served in a scooped out watermelon half with the edges cut in a sawtooth border. I serve it with a chicken or crab casserole. It can also be served as a dessert.

1 cup diced fresh cantaloupe
1 cup diced fresh watermelon
1 cup diced fresh pineapple
1 cup mandarin orange sections
2 cups fresh strawberries
1 cup Thompson Seedless grapes
1 cup California Sauterne

Mix ingredients together — refrigerate and serve cold. The variations on fruit are endless, using any fresh or canned fruit.

My choice of wine to accompany this dish:
CALIFORNIA CHABLIS

Seasoned Wine for Salad Dressing

(1 FIFTH)

Mrs. Walter S. Richert, Richert & Sons, Morgan Hill
This recipe came to me from Lew Largent of Pacific Grove, California, in 1960.

1 Fifth bottle California
   Zinfandel
   Handful of parsley
5 cloves of garlic
   Lemon juice

Remove ¼ of the bottle of wine. (This portion may be consumed while completing this recipe.) Chop parsley, peel and halve garlic cloves; add to wine bottle. Fill remainder of bottle with lemon juice. Seal and store in refrigerator for two weeks before use.

Cream of Mushroom Soup with Sherry

(5 SERVINGS)

Mrs. August Sebastiani, Samuele Sebastiani Winery, Sonoma

¾ pound fresh mushrooms
3 tablespoons butter
3 tablespoons flour
4 cups scalded milk
1 egg yolk
½ cup California Dry Sherry
   Salt and pepper to taste

Slice mushroom caps and chop the stems. Sauté in butter until they are lightly browned, sprinkle with flour, and cook over low heat for 4 minutes. Add milk and simmer the soup, stirring for 10 minutes. Mix egg yolk, lightly beaten, and Sherry and add to the soup. Add salt and pepper to taste and cook soup for 2 minutes longer. Garnish with finely chopped parsley.

My choice of wine to accompany this dish: **CALIFORNIA RED TABLE WINE**

Fruit Salad Dressing

(MAKES 1½ CUPS)

Mrs. Harold Berg, University of California, Department of Viticulture and Enology, Davis

1 cup mayonnaise
½ cup dairy sour cream
2 tablespoons chopped chutney
1 tablespoon capers, drained
1 tablespoon chopped chives
1 tablespoon sliced pimiento
¼ teaspoon curry powder
2 tablespoons California Sherry

Blend all ingredients well and serve with fresh fruit salad, avocado and grapefruit salad or iceberg lettuce.

Editor's note: **CALIFORNIA HAUT SAUTERNE**
is a good complement to this salad.

Appetizer wines have been enjoyed for centuries. And modern day Epicures are finding that they make an excellent start to today's good foods. Their function, now as always, is to alert the appetite for the meal to come. For this, you can count on California dry Sherry, a sweet or dry Vermouth, one of the natural flavored wines or even on a dry Champagne. Mixed wine drinks are still a novelty to many, even though such "house specialties" as Sherry Sour, Vermouth Half-and-Half, wine lemonade, and various wine coolers have been making aperitif history in California for many years. Some additional choice wine drinks are among the recipes in this section. Another way to stimulate the appetite is to offer wine-flavored hors d'oeuvres, canapes, and dips. When accompanied by a before-dinner wine, these appetizers serve as a prelude to the delicious wine and food combinations that follow.

HORS D'OEUVRES
and BEVERAGES

Hors d'oeuvres

Lobster Rumaki

(4 TO 6 SERVINGS)

Mrs. Arthur Caputi, Jr., E. & J. Gallo Winery, Modesto
Editor's note: Rumaki is the favorite cocktail-hour tidbit in the West.
Count on serving several per person when planning a party.

1 (9-oz.) package frozen
    rock lobster tails, thawed
2 tablespoons salad oil
¼ cup soy sauce
¼ cup California Dry Sherry
1 teaspoon lemon peel, grated
    Small piece ginger root, or
    ¼ teaspoon powdered
    ginger
6 or 7 slices bacon, halved
1 small can water chestnuts

Remove lobster meat from shells and cut into 1-inch pieces. Combine salad oil, soy sauce, Sherry, lemon peel and ginger. Add lobster, mix, and refrigerate for at least 1 hour. To assemble, wrap a piece of bacon around a piece of water chestnut and lobster and secure with a pick or bamboo skewer. Broil 4 inches from heat, turning occasionally for 10 minutes or until bacon is crisp. Serve warm. Bacon may also be partially cooked while lobster meat is marinating. For added flavor, drain marinade and simmer until reduced slightly, then brush over cooked lobster.

My choice of wine to accompany this dish:
CALIFORNIA COCKTAIL SHERRY

Blossom Hill Cannibal Canape

Mrs. E. Jeff Barnette, Martini-Prati Winery, Santa Rosa
This is a delicious canape and a conversational dish.

2 pounds choice top grade
    lean ground beef
½ cup finely chopped onion
1 tablespoon Worcestershire
    sauce
3 dashes tabasco
1 teaspoon salt
½ teaspoon freshly ground
    black pepper
1 teaspoon dry mustard
1 clove garlic, crushed
2 egg yolks
⅓ cup California Port or Sherry
1 tablespoon finely cut
    parsley or chives

Mix well chilled beef with all other ingredients. Shape mixture in a fancy mold or bowl. Refrigerate until ready to use. Unmold, surround with thin slices of rye or pumpernickel bread cut into small squares or crisp crackers. Let guests spread their own.

Editor's note: Have plenty of **CALIFORNIA DRY SHERRY**
on hand to go with this appetizer.

73

Lobster Tail Glacé à la Marguerey

(2 SERVINGS)

Mrs. Leon Peters, Valley Foundry, Fresno
We enjoyed this dish served in very small quantities in individual baking dishes as a first course
at the El Tovar Hotel in Grand Canyon.
It is best served as a first course in a small quantity as it is quite rich.

1 whole lobster tail
2 tablespoons butter
4 mushrooms, sliced
  Pinch paprika
2 tablespoons flour
3 tablespoons California
  Dry Sherry
2 cups light cream
  Salt to taste

Boil one whole lobster tail about 10 minutes. Take out of shell and dice, then put butter in skillet and sauté lobster with mushrooms and paprika. Add flour. Add Sherry and light cream and simmer until thick. Salt to taste and pour lobster into individual shells or casseroles, pour warm sauce over and glaze under broiler until brown.

 My choice of wine to accompany this dish: **CALIFORNIA PINOT BLANC**

Oyster Appetizers

(4 TO 5 SERVINGS)

Mrs. Greg Goorigian, Vie-Del Company, Fresno

1 tablespoon lemon juice
2 tablespoons buttery oil
1 tablespoon instant
  minced onion
⅛ teaspoon pepper
½ teaspoon salt
¼ teaspoon dry mustard
¼ cup California Dry Sherry
1 pint fresh oysters
½ pound sliced bacon

Combine lemon juice, oil, onion, pepper, salt, dry mustard and wine. Pour mixture over fresh oysters and refrigerate for 2 to 3 hours, spooning mixture over oysters several times while marinating. Just before cooking, make sure oysters have been generously coated again with mixture extra-large oysters may be cut in half). Then wrap each oyster with ½ slice bacon, secure with toothpick. Put on grate and barbecue over hot coals, or if barbecue is not available use hot broiler. Brown on one side, turn, brown on other side. Serve at once.

 Editor's note: Serve the same **CALIFORNIA DRY SHERRY** *used in the preparation of these appetizers with them.*

Brandied Chicken Liver Paté

Mrs. Philip Smyser, Wine Advisory Board, San Francisco
One recipe of this paté lasts us several months since it is so rich.
I store it in small crocks and serve it as a spread on crackers or toast.

2 pounds chicken livers,
  chopped
½ cup butter
2 medium onions, quartered
1 teaspoon paprika
1 teaspoon curry powder
¼ teaspoon salt
¼ teaspoon pepper
1 cup softened butter
¼ cup California Brandy

Combine in a sauce pan the first 5 ingredients. Cover and cook over low heat for 10 minutes. Puree in a blender or force through sieve. Stir in the softened butter and Brandy. Put the paté in a crock or covered dish and chill until firm.

  My choice of wine to accompany this dish:
  CALIFORNIA DRY SHERRY *or* **DRY VERMOUTH**

Oyster Stuffed Mushroom Caps

(10 TO 12 SERVINGS)

Mrs. Louis P. Martini, Louis M. Martini Winery, St. Helena
I use this as a first course or as an appetizer with a light dry white table wine.

30 large mushrooms
Butter
Lemon juice
1 pint fresh oysters
½ cup California
    White Table Wine
¼ teaspoon horseradish
¼ cup lemon juice
Salt and pepper
1 clove garlic
¼ cup butter

Carefully remove stems and set aside. Clean mushroom caps, being careful not to break. In a covered frying pan melt butter and squeeze in lemon juice. Place mushrooms under side down in the pan, squeeze a small amount of lemon juice over caps and cover and cook slowly until cooked, but not mushy soft. Place bottom side up on a buttered baking dish. Cut fresh oysters in small pieces and fill mushroom caps. In a cup, mix wine, horseradish, lemon juice, salt and pepper and spoon a little over each cap. Clean mushroom stems and grind together through meat grinder (or chop very fine) with one clove of garlic. Blend in softened butter. Put a small amount on each cap. Refrigerate until ready to serve (may be made a few hours ahead of time); 15 minutes before serving, place under broiler and cook until the butter melts and browns.

My choice of wine to accompany this dish:
CALIFORNIA JOHANNISBERG RIESLING

Crab Delight Dip

(TWO CUPS)

Mrs. Shelton Brown, Paul Masson Vineyards, Saratoga
Editor's note: The delicate Sherry flavor in this dip suggests it as suitable to be served with Sherry as an appetizer before dinner. The recipe is also good made with shrimp or lobster.

1 cup mayonnaise
½ cup dairy sour cream
1 tablespoon finely chopped
    parsley
1 (6½-oz.) can crabmeat,
    drained
1 tablespoon California
    Medium Sherry
1 teaspoon lemon juice
Salt and pepper

Combine all ingredients. Chill at least 2 hours before serving. Serve with crackers or crisp, raw vegetables for dipping.

Editor's note: **CALIFORNIA DRY SHERRY** *or* **DRY VERMOUTH** *over ice is perfect with this.*

Cheese Fondue

(10 SERVINGS)

Mrs. Irvine C. Mettler, Woodbridge Vineyard, Lodi
Cheese fondue, served in the classic way with cubes of French bread to dip into the melted cheese mixture, is almost a full meal in itself. Sometimes we add salad and a simple dessert.

Garlic
2 cups California
    White Table Wine
1 pound Swiss cheese
1 pound Jack cheese
4 tablespoons flour
1 tablespoon California Brandy

Rub fondue pot with cut clove of garlic; pour in wine and heat. Dredge cheese in flour and in small amounts, slowly add to wine, stirring constantly. Mixture is ready when thick and smooth. Add Brandy.

My choice of wine to accompany this dish: **CALIFORNIA CHABLIS**

Stuffed Mushroom Missouri

(5 TO 6 SERVINGS)

Dr. Salvatore P. Lucia, University of California, School of Medicine, San Francisco

20 to 30 mushrooms
    Boiling water, salted
1 cup finely ground
    sauteed or roast pork
1 tablespoon diced celery
1 tablespoon pine nuts
1 tablespoon minced chives
2 tablespoons sliced ripe olives
    Salt and pepper
1 egg, beaten
1⅓ tablespoons light cream
2 tablespoons butter
1 tablespoon California Brandy
    Sweet butter
    Sliced lemon peel

Cook mushrooms gently in water until tender, about 5 minutes. Separate stems from caps. Chop stems into fine pieces. Measure 1 cup of mushroom stems. Add pork, celery, pine nuts, chives, and ripe olives. Season to taste with salt and pepper. Moisten with egg and cream mixture, and simmer until celery is tender. Add Brandy. Fill mushroom caps. Top each with a bit of sweet butter, and grill under broiler until lightly browned. Serve with a sliver of lemon peel.

My choice of wine to accompany this dish:
CALIFORNIA BRUT CHAMPAGNE *or* **MUSCAT DE FRONTIGNAN**

San Jose Giblets

(8 TO 10 SERVINGS)

E. A. Mirassou, Mirassou Vineyards, San Jose
This is a delightful hors d'oeuvre.
During cooking time baste the chef internally with the California Sherry or Champagne.

¼ cup butter
1 clove pressed garlic
    Salt and pepper
⅛ teaspoon monosodium
    glutamate
¼ teaspoon thyme
¼ teaspoon sage
2 pounds fresh or frozen
    chicken giblets (gizzards,
    chicken hearts and livers)
¼ cup chopped parsley
½ cup California Sherry
1 cup California Champagne
    or any California Dry
    White Wine will substitute

Melt butter in 10-inch frying pan with garlic, sprinkle ½ the dry spices over giblets. Place them in pan, seasoned side down; then add balance of dry spices to giblets. Sprinkle on parsley. Brown giblets on all sides. Reduce heat and simmer for 20 minutes or until tender. Increase heat. Pour in Sherry rapidly 1 minute later pour in Champagne. Allow to simmer in open fry pan until sauce is reduced by two-thirds. It is now ready to serve. Cut giblets in bite size pieces and serve with cocktail picks.

My Choice of wine to accompany this dish: **CALIFORNIA CHAMPAGNE**

Mushrooms Catalan

(4 TO 5 SERVINGS)

Mrs. Joseph Heitz, Heitz Wine Cellars, St. Helena
Editor's note: An easy and elegant hors d'oeuvre.
Choose small cloves of garlic so the flavor won't be too potent.

1½ pounds firm fresh mushrooms
½ cup olive oil
1 onion, sliced
4 small garlic cloves, sliced
Bouquet garni (several sprigs
   of fresh herbs, such as
   parsley, thyme, basil)
Salt and pepper
½ cup California
   White Table Wine
Finely chopped parsley

Remove stems from mushrooms and reserve for another use. Wash the caps and dry them well. In a skillet heat olive oil, add onion and cook very slowly until onion is soft, but not browned. Add garlic, bouquet garni, salt and pepper, and wine. Heat to simmering. Add mushroom caps. Boil them for 5 minutes. Then remove from heat and allow mushrooms to cool completely in the liquid. Drain the mushrooms and serve them sprinkled with finely chopped parsley as an hors d'oeuvre.

Editor's note: **CALIFORNIA DRY SHERRY, VERMOUTH** *or* **BRUT CHAMPAGNE** *goes well with this hors d'oeuvre.*

Mushrooms Bourguignon

(6 SERVINGS)

Mrs. Cecil P. Kahmann, Wine Institute, San Francisco
You can serve this as a hot appetizer with cocktail picks,
or thicken the wine sauce slightly and serve over steak or chops.

¼ cup butter
1 clove garlic
2 shallots, minced
   (or green onions)
1 pound medium-size
   whole mushrooms
1 cup California Burgundy
1 tablespoon minced parsley
Dash of mace
Salt and freshly ground
   black pepper

Melt butter in skillet and add crushed garlic and minced shallots. Toss a couple of minutes until tender and golden brown. Add mushrooms, wine, parsley and seasonings. Simmer about 5 to 10 minutes. Serve from a chafing dish or other heated buffet server as a hot hors d'oeuvre. Have cocktail picks available, or serve on small plates with forks.

Editor's note: **CALIFORNIA DRY VERMOUTH** *complements this appetizer perfectly.*

Wine Olives

Mrs. Frank Bartholomew, Buena Vista Vineyards, Sonoma
Whenever we were served an aperitif in Portugal or Spain, these wine olives accompanied it.
Editor's note: A jar of these olives can be kept in the refrigerator for use any time.
They make a good relish as well as an appetizer.

Olives
Sherry or Madeira

Put olives, either green or ripe, in a small serving bowl and cover with Sherry or Medeira. Refrigerate at least two hours until thoroughly chilled. Serve from bowl in the middle of a canape tray.

Editor's note: Serve **CALIFORNIA DRY SHERRY** *with these olives for an appetizing combination, or try one of California's Special Natural Wines.*

Beverages

Evergreen Delight

(6 SERVINGS)

Mrs. E. A. Mirassou, Mirassou Vineyards, San Jose
*A warm nightcap for a cool evening, this drink also makes a delightful summer nightcap
when the honey, whipped cream and nutmeg are omitted. Serve it over ice cubes.*

6 jiggers California Brandy
6 tablespoons honey
6 cups hot milk (don't boil)
Whipped cream
Nutmeg

Preheat 6 mugs and add 1 jigger of Brandy to each. Stir honey into milk until dissolved. Pour hot milk mixture into Brandy. If calories don't count, add a squiggle of whipped cream and top with a sprinkle of nutmeg.

A Lion's Kiss

(1 4-OUNCE SERVING)

Fred E. Weibel, Jr., Weibel Champagne Vineyards, Mission San Jose
*Editor's note: A bright and cheerful summer taste treat,
the proportions can be increased to serve as a punch if desired.*

3 ounces California Champagne
1 ounce California
   Tangerine-flavored Wine

To a chilled Champagne glass, add Tangerine-flavored Wine and Champagne. Stir lightly and serve. If desired, garnish with a slice of orange or tangerine.

Winemaker's Champagne Punch

(25 TO 30 SERVINGS)

Mrs. Catherine Menth, California Wine Association, San Francisco
*Various frozen fruit juices can be added to this recipe as desired.
Sometimes I add frozen orange juice concentrate and frozen pink lemonade concentrate.*

1 fifth California
   White Table Wine
1 cup California Brandy
1 fifth California Champagne
1 large bottle (quart) lemon-
   lime carbonated beverage

Pre-chill ingredients. Mix wine and Brandy in punch bowl. Pour Champagne and lemon-lime beverage in punch bowl simultaneously. Serve immediately.

Frosted Fruit Juice

(4 SERVINGS)

Mrs. N. C. Mirassou, Mirassou Vinyards, San Jose
Editor's note: This fruity combination makes a light, refreshing and frothy drink, nice for
mid-afternoon or evening. The natural grape sugar in the Sherry makes it pleasantly sweet.

1 cup orange juice
1 cup California Sweet Sherry
½ cup pineapple juice
½ cup crushed ice
2 egg whites
   Fresh mint sprigs

Combine juices and wine in a shaker with crushed ice. Beat egg white
slightly and add to shaker. Shake until frothy. Strain into glasses garnished
with mint and serve.

Nectar of the Sea

(1 SERVING)

David R. Wilcox, Wine Advisory Board, San Francisco
This was the result of a successful experiment. I have always enjoyed the three
beverages separately and I wondered one day how they would taste together.

¼ cup tomato juice
¼ cup clam juice
½ cup California Rhine Wine

Chill all ingredients well, mix together thoroughly in a glass and garnish
edge with a thick wedge of lemon.

Bombay Punch

(ABOUT 30 SERVINGS)

Mrs. Shelton Brown, Paul Masson Vineyards, Saratoga
Editor's note: This punch has a very pleasant flavor and considerable authority.
When you want to present a truly festive drink for a memorable occasion,
such as a wedding reception, try this one.

1 pint California Brandy
1 pint California Sherry
3 ounces maraschino liqueur
3 ounces Orange Curacao
   Fresh fruits for garnish
1 quart carbonated water
2 quarts California Champagne

Mix Brandy, Sherry and liqueurs in punch bowl with large block of ice.
Garnish with slices of fresh fruit. Add carbonated water and Champagne
just before serving.

Rosé Fruit Punch

(16 4-OUNCE SERVINGS)

Mrs. John Franzia, Sr., Franzia Brothers Winery, Ripon
Editor's note: This light, pitcher punch refreshes marvelously on a warm afternoon.

4 cups California Vin Rosé
4 cups fresh or frozen
   grapefruit juice
4 tablespoons grenadine syrup

Combine all ingredients and chill thoroughly. Makes 2 quarts of punch.

A glass of dessert wine is the sweet way to end an Epicurean meal. Sometimes it is paired with fresh fruit and nuts, sometimes with cheese. There's great variety in each of these foods, so the combination can be new every time. Among the wines, there are Port, Sweet Sherry, several Muscats, Angelica and Tokay. These are heavy bodied, rich in flavor and color. Another group, perhaps less well known, are the light sweet wines such as Haut Sauterne or its varietal counterparts Sweet Semillon and Sweet Sauvignon Blanc. Light sweet muscats are fruity and delicious, and sweet Champagne, either pink or the more familiar pale golden, ends a meal in style. We Americans like "made" desserts, and here, too, wine can play an important role as the recipes in this section prove.

DESSERTS

Classic Zuppa Inglese

(16 TO 20 SERVINGS)

Mrs. Robert Diana, Villa Armando, Pleasanton

Zuppa Inglese (English Soup) probably has more variations and stories about its origin than any other Italian food including macaroni. When Eighteenth-Century English tourists went to Italy they grew nostalgic for their trifle (Tipsy Cake). So Italian cooks tried to please them by soaking sponge cake with rum or Sherry. There was a great deal of the liquid, so much so that it had to be eaten with a spoon. They referred to the cake, among themselves, as a soup— "English Soup." Some stories say that the Zuppa was first served to Lord Nelson and Lady Hamilton. I reserve this dessert for special occasions such as for a birthday, graduation party or even for a bridal party. To serve it, I cut a large circle in the center and cut the outer ring into serving pieces first.

9 eggs
1½ cups sugar
1½ teaspoons vanilla
1½ cups self-rising flour, sifted
4 tablespoons cornstarch
1 cup sugar
    Pinch of salt
4 cups milk
6 egg yolks, slightly beaten
1 ounce baking chocolate, melted
½ cup California Cream Sherry
1 pint whipping cream
    Sugar
    Vanilla
¼ cup California Cream Sherry
    Candied cherries

In large bowl of electric mixer, combine eggs, 1½ cups sugar and 1½ teaspoons vanilla and beat at high speed for not less than 20 minutes, until lemon colored. With spatula fold in sifted flour ¼ cup at a time. Place equal amounts of batter in four 8-inch cake pans that have been lightly greased and floured. Bake in moderate oven (350°) for 20 minutes, or until sides of cake shrink from pans. Cool 10 minutes on racks, then remove from pans. Meanwhile, make fillings. In top of double boiler, mix cornstarch, 1 cup sugar and salt. Add milk and egg yolks; set over boiling water; cook, stirring constantly, until thickened. Divide the filling in half. To one half, add melted chocolate and blend thoroughly. Cool fillings thoroughly, then add ¼ cup Sherry to each. Whip the cream until peaks form when you raise the beaters. Flavor to taste with sugar and vanilla. Set aside. To assemble the cake, sprinkle an additional ¼ cup Sherry evenly over the 4 layers. Spread first layer with half the chocolate filling; second layer with the white filling; third, with remaining chocolate, and fourth, with the remaining white filling. Directly on top of the white filling place some of the whipped cream, then cover the sides also. Decorate the top and sides by forcing the remainder of the whipped cream through pastry bag and No. 27 star decorating tip. Garnish with candied cherries. Refrigerate for several hours or even overnight before serving.

Editor's note: **CALIFORNIA MEDIUM SWEET CHAMPAGNE** *is the perfect beverage to go with this dessert.*

Macaroon Trifle

(4 OR 5 SERVINGS)

Mrs. August Sebastiani, Samuele Sebastiani Winery, Sonoma
This recipe comes from a good friend, Mrs. Mark Pasquini of San Francisco, who is one of
the greatest Epicurean cooks I know. We enjoy sharing our recipes.
I have served this dessert with a great variety of menus.

¼ **pound almond macaroons**
¼ **pound ladyfingers**
½ **cup raspberry jam**
    Custard sauce (below)
¼ **cup California**
    Medium Sherry
¼ **cup California Brandy**
    Maraschino cherries
    Whipped cream
    CUSTARD SAUCE
2 **tablespoons cornstarch**
2 **cups milk**
3 **tablespoons sugar**
3 **egg yolks**
3 **tablespoons water**

Use a small bowl (about 6-cup size). Break macaroons and ladyfingers in
two and mix together. Line bowl with part of jam. Add part of cakes to
lining of bowl. Spread with remaining jam. Add wine and Brandy to custard sauce and whip all 3 together. Add custard sauce to the remainder of
the cakes, and fill the bowl. Cover and refrigerate overnight. Just before
serving, decorate with maraschino cherries and whipped cream. **Custard
Sauce:** Blend cornstarch with ½ cup cold milk. Heat 1½ cups milk in
double boiler, stir in cornstarch mixture. Beat together the sugar, egg
yolks and water. Add hot milk, stirring constantly. Cook 5 to 10 minutes
to a thin custard consistency. Cool and use as directed above.

 My choice of wine to accompany this dish: **CALIFORNIA CHAMPAGNE**

Cenci

(8 DOZEN)

Mrs. Joe Carrari, Paul Masson Vineyards, Soledad
Cenci may be served with most any type of dessert in place of cake or cookies.
They are excellent served with wine for guests.

4 **cups unsifted cake flour**
¼ **cup butter or margarine**
⅓ **cup granulated sugar**
4 **eggs**
½ **cup California**
    Cream Sherry
    Salad oil or shortening
    for deep-frying
    Powdered sugar

Place flour in a large bowl. With pastry blender, cut in butter until mixture resembles coarse crumbs. Then stir in granulated sugar. In small
bowl, lightly beat eggs with Sherry. Add to flour mixture, stirring until all
flour is moistened. On lightly floured surface, knead dough until smooth
(about 5 minutes). Cover, and let rest 10 minutes. In deep-fat fryer or
heavy saucepan, slowly heat salad oil (4 inches deep) to 400° on deep-
frying thermometer. Meanwhile, cut off one-sixth of dough at a time, and
roll to paper thinness. With pastry cutter or knife, cut into strips 8 inches
long and ¾ inch wide; tie some into knots by making a small cut in center
of strips, then lacing one end through and pulling gently into knot. If
desired, cut some into 2-inch diamonds. Gently drop dough shapes, a few
at a time, into hot oil, and cook 1 minute, or until very lightly browned.
With slotted utensil, lift out of oil, and drain on paper towels. Let cool.
Sprinkle with powdered sugar. May be stored, loosely covered, in dry
place.

 *My choice of wine to accompany cenci: Any California dessert wine
such as* **CALIFORNIA SWEET SHERRY, PORT,** *or* **MUSCATEL**

Sherry Savarin

(10 TO 12 SERVINGS)

Mrs. Louis P. Martini, Louis M. Martini Winery, St. Helena

SAVARIN
4 eggs
¾ cup sugar
1 teaspoon salt
2 packages dry yeast dissolved in ¾ cup warm milk
2 cups flour
1 cube butter melted
1 cup flour
SAUCE
1 (11-oz.) can Mandarin orange segments
1 cup California Sherry
Water
1 cup sugar
GLAZE
1½ cup apricot jam
Flaked coconut (optional)
FILLING
1½ pints whipping cream
Sugar
Sherry

Savarin: Beat eggs until light, add sugar and salt and beat. Add dissolved yeast and milk mixture. Beat in 2 cups flour until batter is glossy. Add melted butter and 1 cup flour and beat until batter is stiff, but not stiff enough to work by hand. Let mixture raise until double in bulk. Beat down and put in mold (I use a large Bundt pan) and let raise again until double. Bake in hot oven (425°) for 30 to 40 minutes. If getting too brown, lower heat to 375°. Yeast doughs are cooked when they sound hollow to a rap with the knuckles. **Sauce:** Drain the juice from Mandarin orange slices into measuring pitcher (reserve orange sections for later) add Sherry and enough water to make 2½ cups liquid. Bring to a rapid boil and add sugar. Boil 1 or 2 minutes after sugar dissolves. Cool to lukewarm. Prick Savarin with a fork and spoon sauce over cake letting it soak in. First prick bottom of cake and spoon about ⅓ of sauce over it. Then carefully turn and place on serving plate and spoon rest of sauce over top. Let stand 12 hours at room temperature. If sauce drains out of cake, carefully spoon back over cake. **Glaze:** After cake has set for 12 hours, melt apricot jam and put through sieve and spread over cake. Flaked coconut may be sprinkled over top. **Filling:** Just before serving, whip cream until stiff, flavor with sugar and Sherry to taste. Fold in reserved Mandarin orange sections (well drained) and fill center of cake with this mixture. Serve any extra whipped cream mixture separately in bowl.

 My choice of wine to accompany this dish:
CALIFORNIA SPARKLING MUSCAT

California Crepes Suzette

(4 SERVINGS)

Marc and Ze've Halperin, The Christian Brothers, Reedley
Long considered the dessert of sophisticated upper classes, Crepes Suzette are fast becoming part of the menu of the average household. For convenience, crepes may be made in advance and frozen, if necessary.

CREPES
1 cup sifted flour
2 eggs
1¼ cups milk
Butter

SAUCE
4 tablespoons butter
¼ cup sugar
1 teaspoon strained lemon juice
¾ cup strained orange juice
½ cup California Light Sweet Muscat
4 tablespoons California Brandy

Crepes: Prepare batter with the flour, eggs and milk. Beat until perfectly smooth. Pour into a hot, buttered frying pan to cover bottom; pour back excess. (Pan should be hot enough so that batter sizzles). Allow to cook till crepe is brown, then flip over to brown on the other side. Crepes should be as thin as possible. As they are finished, fold into quarters and place in chafing dish or large frying pan. (Butter frying pan as needed.) **Sauce:** Melt butter in medium-hot sauce pan. Sprinkle in sugar. Using a wire blender, mix continuously until sugar is slightly browned. Remove from heat, immediately add the lemon and orange juices. Put back on heat and continue blending till sugar is completely dissolved. Add the wine and Brandy, blending thoroughly. Pour over crepes. To serve: Place chafing dish with crepes over high heat and spoon sauce over crepes until sauce bubbles. Put 4 tablespoons Brandy into a ladle, warm Brandy by setting ladle in hot water, then ignite Brandy and pour over the crepes.

 Our choice of wine to accompany this dish: **CALIFORNIA CREAM SHERRY**

Brandy Mince Meat

(12 SERVINGS)

Mrs. Alvin Ehrhardt, United Vintners, San Francisco
Use this mince meat as the filling for a lattice-top pie.
It is especially good served warm with a fluffy Sherry hard sauce.
Editor's note: A quart container of mince meat will make two 9-inch pies if the mince meat is
mixed with an equal amount of chopped fresh apple. To freeze the filling for one pie
without adding any other fruit, put only 3 cups of mince meat into the quart container.

MINCE MEAT
2 pounds boneless beef
    stew meat cubed
1 pound beef suet,
    membrane removed
1 pound candied fruit peel
3 pounds apples, pared,
    cored and chopped
2 pounds light brown sugar
4 cups cider
1 tablespoon salt
1 tablespoon nutmeg
1 tablespoon allspice
1 tablespoon cloves
2 tablespoons cinnamon
1½ cups light molasses
3 (11-oz.) packages currants
1 pound each seedless raisins
    and golden raisins
2 cups California Brandy

SHERRY HARD SAUCE
½ cup butter or margarine
2½ cups sifted powdered sugar
⅛ teaspoon cinnamon
¼ cup California Sherry

Mince Meat: Cover meat with water and bring to a boil, cook until tender and almost dry, about 1½ hours. Cool and put through food chopper using medium blade. (You should have 5½ cups of ground cooked meat.) Put suet and candied fruit peel through the chopper. Mix with meat and apples. Dissolve sugar in cider in large pan, bring to a boil. Add meat mixture carefully and return to a boil. Reduce heat and simmer 5 minutes. Remove from heat. Add salt, spices, molasses, currants and raisins, mix thoroughly. Blend in Brandy, cool to room temperature. **Sherry Hard Sauce:** Beat butter or margarine until creamy. Beat in sifted powdered sugar and cinnamon alternately with Sherry. Beat until mixture forms stiff, creamy peaks. Makes 2 cups sauce. Or add Sherry to taste to commercially prepared Hard Sauce sold in jars.

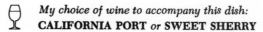 *My choice of wine to accompany this dish:*
CALIFORNIA PORT *or* **SWEET SHERRY**

Strawberry Cardinal Topping

(6 TO 8 SERVINGS)

Mrs. Charles J. Welch, Guild Wine Company, San Francisco
This topping may be served over ice cream, or over plain cake—
unfrosted angel food, pound, or such.

1½ quarts fresh strawberries (or
    whole frozen may be
    substituted)
¼ to ⅓ cup sugar (omit if
    frozen berries are used)
1 (10-oz.) package frozen
    raspberries
2 tablespoons California
    Brandy
1 teaspoon lemon juice

Wash and hull fresh strawberries. Cut into bite-size pieces. Place in a bowl and sprinkle with sugar. Cover and chill. Thaw raspberries. Blend in electric blender until thoroughly pureed and slightly frothy. Strain. Stir in the Brandy and lemon juice. Drain excess liquid from strawberries. Blend raspberry mixture and berries.

My choice of wine to accompany this dish: **CALIFORNIA ROSÉ** *or*
WHITE TABLE WINE, *depending on the meat course.*

Plum Wine Jelly

(6 TO 8 SERVINGS)

Mrs. Edmund Accomazzo, Cucamonga Winery, Cucamonga
Editor's note: This dessert makes a soft jelly, not firm. The consistency is part of its charm.
To make a jelly that will hold its shape, reduce the water to 1½ cups.

2 cups sliced purple or
   red plums
1 cup honeydew melon balls
2 cups water
5 whole cloves
1 stick cinnamon, broken
½ lemon sliced
1 (3-oz.) package strawberry
   gelatin
2 teaspoons lemon juice
¾ cup California Tokay

Combine sliced plums and melon balls in a shallow dessert bowl. In a saucepan, combine 1 cup water, cloves, cinnamon and lemon and bring to a boil. Add gelatin and stir until dissolved. Add remaining 1 cup water, lemon juice and wine. Pour over plums and melon balls in bowl. Chill until set. Spoon into dessert glasses and, if desired, top with whipped cream.

Editor's note: The wine used in the preparation of this dish, **CALIFORNIA TOKAY,** *is a delicious accompaniment.* **CALIFORNIA PORT** *is also excellent.*

Grand Sherry Chocolate Mousse

(6 SERVINGS)

Mrs. Frank Franzia, Jr., Franzia Brothers Winery, Ripon
This grand dessert recipe was taken a few years ago from a magazine. It was said to be
Raymond Burr's favorite holiday dessert. However, I replaced the liquor it called for with a
California Sherry so a minor change in the name was then necessary.

1 (12-oz.) jar chocolate or
   fudge sauce
1 envelope unflavored gelatin
¼ cup cold water
1 teaspoon instant coffee
   powder
¼ cup California Sweet Sherry
½ pint whipping cream

The day before or early on the day of serving, in saucepan, heat chocolate or fudge sauce, but do not boil. Soften gelatin in cold water; heat over hot water, until dissolved. Stir in hot sauce. Refrigerate in bowl until cool, about 15 minutes. Dissolve instant coffee powder in Sherry and add to above mixture. Then gently fold it into heavy cream, whipped stiff. Spoon into 6 sherbet glasses; refrigerate until served; garnish with unsweetened whipped cream, if desired. This dessert may also be molded.

 My choice of wine to accompany this dish: **CALIFORNIA CHAMPAGNE**

Sauterne Delight

(8 TO 10 SERVINGS)

Mrs. Frank Lico, San Martin Vineyards Company, San Martin
This is a rather rich cake so it should be served with a simple meal such as baked chicken,
green vegetable and oil-vinegar salad. I tried this on my husband's family
and it was accepted rather well, so it must be good.

1 large angel food cake
⅔ cup California Sauterne
1 pint dairy sour cream
1 cup powdered sugar
1 (8-oz.) package cream cheese
   (at room temperature)

Cut cake crosswise in 2 layers. With a long-pronged fork or ice pick, punch about 20 holes in bottom layer. Sprinkle half the wine over that layer. Combine sour cream and sugar. Spread half the mixture on bottom layer of cake. Cover with top layer and sprinkle on remaining wine. Blend remaining cream mixture with cream cheese to make frosting. Spread on top and sides. Chill.

 My choice of wine to accompany this dish:
CALIFORNIA SAUTERNE *or* **SWEET SAUTERNE**

Apple-Brandy Cake

(9 TO 10 SERVINGS)

Mrs. Paul L. Halpern, United Vintners, Madera

1 large egg
1¾ cups chopped raw
    unpeeled apples
1 cup sugar
¼ cup California Brandy
1¼ cups chopped walnuts
¼ cup oil
1 cup sifted cake flour
½ teaspoon nutmeg
1 teaspoon soda
½ teaspoon salt

Beat the egg and stir in the apples to coat them. Add sugar. Add Brandy and nuts. Stir in the oil. Sift remaining dry ingredients together, then sift into the batter and stir until well mixed. Line an 8″ square pan with wax paper and pour in the cake, spreading evenly. Bake in moderate oven (350°) for 40 minutes—or until a pick inserted in cake comes out clean.

 My choice of wine to accompany this dish:
CALIFORNIA CHAMPAGNE *or* **PINK CHABLIS**
Editor's note: For delicious variations, substitute California Sherry or Muscatel for the Brandy in this recipe.

Biscote

(3 DOZEN)

Mrs. Leon Kirschenmann, East-Side Winery, Lodi

3 eggs, well beaten
1 cup sugar
¼ cup California Brandy
2 cups sifted flour
2 teaspoons baking powder
½ teaspoon salt
¼ cup whole anise seed,
    washed in cold water
1 cup coarsely chopped
    almonds
1 teaspoon vanilla
½ cup butter, melted

Beat eggs until light and lemon colored. Add sugar slowly and continue beating. Add Brandy alternately with sifted dry ingredients to which anise seed and almonds have been added. Add vanilla and melted butter. Beat well. Pour ½ inch of batter into small disposable foil bread pans which have been oiled and floured. Bake in moderate oven (350°) until lightly browned on top and batter pulls away from sides of pans—about 20 to 25 minutes. Turn out on board to cool. When cool, slice loaves in ¼-inch slices, arrange slices on unoiled cookie sheets and toast in 300° oven until crisp and lightly browned. Store in tight container. I usually freeze part of the little loaves and toast them as I wish to serve them.

My choice of wine to accompany this dish:
CALIFORNIA CREAM SHERRY *or* **MARSALA**

Chadeau en Tasse Wein

(5 TO 6 SERVINGS)

Mrs. Donald Gregg, Guild Wine Company, Ukiah

½ cup California White Wine
    or California Sherry
    or Angelica
1½ tablespoons sugar
2 whole eggs or 3 egg yolks
1 small piece lemon rind

Mix all ingredients in upper part of double boiler. Set upper part on top of lower part of boiler with hot water, heat gently. Whip vigorously with egg beater until mixture comes just to the boiling point, when all should be foam. (If it boils, it will curdle and the foam will disappear again.) Pick out lemon rind and serve the wine foam immediately in teacups with a cookie or some cake. Or whip it after it is foamy until cold again. In that case use 3 yolks and add 1 white of egg, beaten stiff, before serving. If used as a pudding sauce, increase wine to 1 cup with the same ingredients. It also goes well with rice, prunes and bread pudding.

 Editor's note: **A CALIFORNIA SWEET SAUTERNE** *or* **LIGHT SWEET MUSCAT** *is a pleasant accompaniment for a pudding topped with this "wine foam."*

Chocolate Muscatel Peaches

(6 TO 8 SERVINGS)

Mrs. John Franzia, Sr., Franzia Brothers Winery, Ripon
This recipe is one my mother-in-law gave me years ago. It is truly something very scrumptious to serve during the fresh peach season, especially for a Sunday dinner.
Our menu then usually includes chicken with ravioli or spaghetti.

10 freestone peaches, slightly ripened, fresh, firm, medium yellow, unpeeled
2 cups California Muscatel
18 Italian almond macaroons, crumbled (1⅓ cup crumbs)
⅓ cup sugar
1 egg, beaten
⅓ cup ground chocolate
1 teaspoon vanilla
5 chopped peach pit kernels

Cut peaches in half. With a melon baller or a teaspoon measure, enlarge the cavity in each half slightly to hold the filling. Reserve the pulp scooped out. Arrange peaches in bowl. Pour wine over peaches and allow to marinate for about ½ hour. Meanwhile, make the filling: Crush macaroons, add sugar, beaten egg, ground chocolate, vanilla and reserved peach pulp. Crack peach pits, remove kernel, chop and add to filling. Remove peaches from wine; place in lightly buttered baking dish. Place a mound of filling mixture in the cavity of each peach half. (Mixture should be thick; if too soft add more macaroon crumbs.) Bake in moderate oven (350°) until browned, about 40 minutes. Serve hot or cold.

Editor's note: **CALIFORNIA LIGHT, SWEET MUSCAT** *is delightful with this dessert.*

Bulgarian Brandied Fruit

(6 SERVINGS)

Mrs. Donald Gregg, Guild Wine Company, Ukiah
I serve this fresh fruit mixture either as a dessert or as an appetizer.

1 large pear
1 large apple
1 large orange
2 medium peaches
2 cups cubed melon
1 cup grapes or fresh cherries
½ cup powdered sugar
¾ cup California White Table Wine
¼ cup lemon juice
¼ to ⅓ cup California Brandy

About three hours before serving, cut pear, apple, orange sections and peaches into cubes or slices, arrange in a pretty glass bowl together with melon and grapes. Add sugar, wine and lemon juice, blending well. Refrigerate until serving time. Just before serving, toss fruit with Brandy.

Editor's note: To complement this dish, serve a **CALIFORNIA SWEET SAUTERNE** *or* **MEDIUM SWEET CHAMPAGNE.**

Curried Fruit Compote

(8 SERVINGS)

Mrs. Jack Farrior, Jr., Almaden Vineyards, Los Gatos
Editor's note: This attractive dessert can be served warm or cold.
The blend of flavors is excellent.

1 (No. 2) can pineapple
1 (No. 2) can pears
1 (No. 2) can peaches
½ cup brown sugar (packed)
¼ cup butter, melted
2 teaspoons curry powder
¼ cup California Sauterne

Place fruits and juices in shallow baking dish and cover with remaining ingredients. Bake for ½ hour at 350°.

 My choice of wine to accompany this dish: **CALIFORNIA CHAMPAGNE**

Dessert Cream Cheese

(4 TO 5 SERVINGS)

Mrs. Philo P. Biane, Brookside Vineyard Company, Guasti

1 (8-oz.) package cream cheese
1 cup powdered sugar
½ cup California Dry Sherry or
   ¼ cup California Brandy
1 egg

In a blender mix cheese, sugar and Sherry or Brandy. Add one whole egg and finish blending at high speed. Pour mixture into small dessert dishes or into lightly oiled small mold. Chill well. This dessert chills to a fairly firm consistency. It can be gently unmolded and surrounded with fruit.

 Editor's note: **A CALIFORNIA LIGHT MUSCAT** or **MEDIUM-SWEET CHAMPAGNE** *complements this dish perfectly.*

Sparkling Champagne Strawberries

(6 SERVINGS)

Mrs. Stephanie DeWitt, Almaden Vineyards, Paicines

2 quarts large strawberries
   Sugar
1 tablespoon Kirschwasser
1 tablespoon Cointreau
2 cups California Sec
   Champagne
1 tablespoon California
   Brandy

Stem strawberries. Do not wash as this softens the berries. Rinse away any dirt with California white table wine, drying each strawberry immediately with paper towel. Sprinkle liberally with sugar; chill. Add liqueurs shortly before serving. Just as serving begins, add the Champagne and Brandy.

 My choice of wine to accompany this dish: **CALIFORNIA SEC CHAMPAGNE**

Port Pudding

(6 TO 8 SERVINGS)

Mrs. Otto Gramlow, Beaulieu Vineyard, Rutherford
This recipe has been handed down from my great grandmother who was a pioneer in California.

2 packages unflavored gelatin
2 cups California Port
2 cups sugar
2 cups water
   Cream or whipped cream

Soften gelatin in ½ cup wine. Combine all ingredients in saucepan and heat until gelatin dissolves. Pour into sherbet or dessert glasses and chill in the refrigerator until set. Serve with thin cream or unsweetened whipped cream. Sherry or Muscat de Frontignan may be substituted for the Port wine.

 Editor's note: **CALIFORNIA HAUT SAUTERNE** *makes a marvelous accompaniment to this dessert.*

Sherried Gelatin Dessert

(4 SERVINGS)

Mrs. John Franzia, Sr., Franzia Brothers Winery, Ripon

1 cup boiling water
1 (3-oz.) package orange-
   pineapple-flavored gelatin
½ cup cold water
½ cup California Dry Sherry

In a mixing bowl, add boiling water to gelatin. Stir to dissolve completely. Add cold water and Sherry. Pour into one layer mold or four individual molds. Chill until set. For variation, add sliced bananas or ½ cup of drained cocktail fruit.

Editor's note: **CALIFORNIA SWEET SAUTERNE** or **LIGHT MUSCAT** *makes an excellent accompanying beverage for this dessert.*

Delicious Sherry Cream Pie

(8 TO 10 SERVINGS)

Mrs. Suzanne McKethen, Wine Advisory Board, San Francisco
This is not an original or family recipe. My mother, Mrs. G. W. Scott, copied it from a
magazine about 25 years ago and she has never found anyone who is familiar with it.

1½ cups crisp chocolate
    cookies, crushed
½ cup butter, melted
1 envelope unflavored gelatin
¼ cup cold milk
3 eggs, separated
½ cup sugar
1 cup milk
⅛ teaspoon salt
¼ teaspoon nutmeg
½ cup California Sherry
½ pint whipping cream

Crush cookies on waxed paper with rolling pin until very fine. Mix with melted butter and pat mixture firmly into 10-inch glass pie plate up over edges to form pie shell. It should not be sticky, only moist. Chill 1 hour. Soften gelatin in cold milk. Put egg yolks in top of double boiler, beat slightly, then add sugar, 1 cup milk; stir well and cook 10 minutes or until mixture coats spoon. Remove from heat. Add gelatin mixture, salt and nutmeg to egg custard, stir until gelatin is dissolved. Add Sherry, very slowly, stirring constantly (if you add Sherry too fast mixture might curdle). Place custard in refrigerator to thicken. When thick, beat egg whites stiff and whip cream firm. Fold egg whites into mixture then add whipped cream to mixture. Pour into chilled, firm piecrust and sprinkle top with grated sweet chocolate or crushed cookies. Chill at least 8 hours or over night.

 Editor's note: A glass of **CALIFORNIA CREAM SHERRY** *complements this dessert beautifully.*

Wine Vinegar Cookies

(TO 10 DOZEN)

Mrs. R. Michael Mondavi, Robert Mondavi Winery, Oakville

1 cup butter
1 cup sugar
1 egg, beaten
3 tablespoons unflavored
    red wine vinegar
3 cups sifted flour
1 teaspoon nutmeg
½ teaspoon baking soda

Set oven temperature for 375°. Cream butter; gradually add sugar and cream well. Mix egg with vinegar and add to creamed mixture. Sift dry ingredients together and gradually add to creamed mixture. Fill cookie press; chill for a few minutes. Form cookies on ungreased cookie sheets. Bake 8 to 10 minutes. Cookies are done when they begin to brown at edges.

 Editor's note: **CALIFORNIA SWEET SHERRY** *or* **PORT** *complements these cookies very well.*

Tutti Fruitti

Mrs. Dinsmoor Webb, University of California, Department of Viticulture and Enology, Davis
This is a recipe given to me by my mother and it had been handed down to her by her mother.

In a heavy crock which has a close-fitting cover, combine equal parts of cut-up fresh fruit, sugar and Brandy. Store in a cool place and stir from time to time. Additional fruit, sugar and Brandy can be added at any time. This compote can be begun with the first Spring strawberries and other fruits added as the season progresses. It is delicious served over ice cream or a cream pudding. It can continue over years to become more complicated in flavor if it is operated on a solera system of each season adding fresh ingredients to replace the amounts removed for consumption.

 Editor's note: Any **CALIFORNIA DESSERT WINE** *or* **CHAMPAGNE** *is excellent with this Brandied fruit.*

A Cellar in Your Home

Imagine being able to say to a guest, "Would you like to come with me to the wine cellar and help me choose the wine for dinner." There's a conversational gambit that stimulates curiosity and heightens anticipation of the meal. Since a wine cellar is so easy to set up, why not have the fun of inviting your guests to participate in the wine selection under your guidance.

Showing off your wine cellar is only part of the fun. Maintaining a stock of wines can enrich your life in many other ways. You always have something elegant and in good taste to serve guests who drop in unexpectedly. There is no need to rush to the store for refreshments. And when you buy wine by the case ahead of time, you save money as well as time. Think of your wine cellar as an extension of your food shelf, and you always have a stock of gourmet ingredients on hand for your cooking.

When you want to give a gift that reflects personal interest and thoughtful selection, choose one or more bottles of wine from your cellar. Champagne, for instance, makes a perfect wedding gift. Some wine cellar owners have cards or labels printed up with their names under the phrase "From the private cellar of . . ." When you present a bottle of wine from your own cellar you give something of yourself.

A wine cellar continually brings you the personal satisfactions of discovery. In trying different wines you discover which ones suit you best. You discover which are the best buys, and you discover which ones age the best. The most practical way to determine how well your favorite wines age is to keep a wine cellar log. Key each bottle of wine, and then on a log sheet or in a log book keep track of when the wine was purchased, and when it was opened and consumed. You might even make notes on how it tasted when you opened it. This will provide you with a guide for future purchases.

How To Start

You can start a wine cellar for as little as $15.00.* A trial selection could include 1 bottle each of the following: a dry or cocktail Sherry; a cream (sweet) Sherry or Port; a dry Vermouth; a Burgundy or similar type (such as Pinot Noir, Gamay, Red Pinot); a Claret or similar type (such as Cabernet, Zinfandel, Grignolino); a Rosé; a Rhine Wine or similar type (such as Johannisberg Riesling, Traminer, Sylvaner); a dry Sauterne or similar type (such as dry Semillon, dry Sauvignon Blanc); a sweet or Haut Sauterne or a light Muscat type; and a medium dry or very dry Champagne. In addition, you should have a half-gallon jug of Sherry for cooking or everyday refreshment. In fact, you can save money by buying other wines in half-gallon and gallon sizes and then decanting them into smaller bottles for easy use. Many excellent wines come in these larger sizes.

* Brand selection, state taxes, transportation and other variables will raise or lower cost.

Where to Locate Your Cellar

Now that you have a fine stock of wine, where do you store it? There are only two requirements for the safe storage of wines that are pure and stable as are all California wines. The storage area must not be subject to constant, strong light and it must have a relatively stable temperature. This is why cellars are perfect for wine storage.

Strong, constant light, particularly sunlight, can harm wine. But note the qualifying word "constant." A couple of days in sunlight will not harm wine, so don't be afraid to take it on picnics or other outings. But for lengthy storage, wine should be kept in a dark area.

Wide fluctuations in temperature can also be harmful to wine. Consequently, the stability of the temperature where the wine is stored is more important than at which temperature it is stored. However a fluctuation of a few degrees will not hurt it. Any temperature in the range from 50 degrees to 60 degrees Farenheit is ideal for storing wine. But wine can be safely stored in temperatures up to 70 degrees. If the temperature rises slightly above 70 degrees for a couple of hours or so on a warm, sunny afternoon there is no cause for alarm. The temperature of wine does not change as readily as air, so the wine will not be harmed.

A wine cellar should provide for the storage of bottles on their sides and standing up. Corked bottles should be stored on their sides to keep the corks moist. This prevents the corks from drying out, shrinking and letting air into the bottle. Metal or plastic enclosed bottles can be stored either upright or on their sides. But having a place to store bottles upright will allow you to include the economical half-gallon and gallon bottles as well as screw-capped fifth bottles.

Wine racks can be purchased in various sizes and at various prices starting at about $4.00. But if you're the resourceful type, you can have fun building your own wine rack; one that fits your special requirements. If you want to improvise, there are many ways to do so. For instance, if you buy a case of wine, stand the case on its side and it makes an excellent wine rack. Cut the ends out of 56-ounce juice cans, fit them snugly between the two sides of a cupboard or cabinet and you have a safe and unique wine rack. Heavy duty mailing tubes can be used the same way. A similar approach is to use agricultural tile. It has the advantage of being a highly efficient insulator which will keep your wine at a more even temperature.

Many modern homes do not have walk-in basements. But this need not prevent your having a wine cellar, because closets, cabinets, lockers, cupboards, and drawers make excellent wine cellars. All that is required is that the storage area protect the wine from light and have a relatively cool and stable temperature.

As you can see there are many ways to obtain a wine "cellar." The important thing to remember is that you are the judge; you choose the wines that you like best. You decide how many bottles best suit your needs. And you decide what kind of "cellar" is the most practical for you.

KITCHEN NOTES

Wine Flavor

Wine is used moderately in the recipes in this book to blend with other ingredients so no one flavor dominates. However, the many who enjoy a more pronounced wine flavor can accomplish this by adding wine to a dish just before it is served.

Also, a bottle called a "wine shaker" with perforated top like a salt shaker can be placed on the table to allow guests to season their food with wine to suit their own tastes. Some hosts give their guests a choice by providing two kinds of wine in table shakers, a Sherry and a red or a white wine.

What Happens to Alcohol In Cooking?

Alcohol boils at a lower temperature (172°) than water. Consequently, when wine is used in cooking, the alcohol evaporates rapidly (in 10 minutes at the simmering temperature), leaving behind the unique flavor and rich aroma of the wine to enhance the food.

Flaming Dishes

Part of the enjoyment of Epicurean cooking is the visual effect. One of the most spectacular ways to present a dish, as well as add to its flavor, is to flame it with Brandy.

For good flaming Brandy, 100-proof is better than 80-proof Brandy. Warm briefly in a double boiler or in a ladle held in a sauce pan of simmering water. Never hold Brandy over direct heat. Pour or ladle gently over the dish and light. A few drops of lemon or orange extract on a sugar cube placed in center of dish with Brandy aids lighting—apply the match to the sugar cube and spoon Brandy gently over resulting flame.

A Good Tenderizer

Many recipes call for marinating foods in wine. With meats wine both flavors and tenderizes. Glass, porcelain, or stainless steel containers are best. Avoid marinating in aluminum containers since it might affect the taste. However, foods can be cooked with wine in aluminum with no adverse effect.

Substitution

Dry table wines are generally interchangeable when used in cooking so long as one white table wine is substituted for another or a red table wine for a different type of red. For instance, if a recipe calls for a Sauterne, and you have only Chablis in the house, there is no reason why the Chablis cannot be used. This is not true of dessert and appetizer wines such as Port and Sherry, however. Substitution of wine in these classes will cause flavor variations in the dish.

Rebottling

Because of their low alcoholic content, table wines are perishable once opened. The best way to prevent spoilage of left-over table wine is to decant it into sterilized smaller bottles leaving not more than an inch and a half of air space at the top. Many wines are sold in the tenth-gallon (12.8 oz.) and fifth gallon (25.6 oz.) sizes with either screw caps or corks. These bottles are ideal for keeping wine left over from larger bottles. If corks are used, they should be tested to see that they don't leak.

Wine Glasses

California's winegrowers recommend an all-purpose, tulip-shaped, nine-ounce, stemmed glass for any wine type. It should be perfectly clear to let the color of the wine show through.

Index of Recipes by Category

Alphabetical Index of Recipes